DIANE SAMUELS

Diane Samuels was born in Liverpool in 1960, and after reading History at Cambridge, went on to train as a drama teacher at Goldsmiths' College, London. She taught in Inner London secondary schools for five years and now writes full-time, living in London with her husband and two sons. Her work for the theatre includes: *The Life and Death of Bessie Smith* (with Sara Milne and Homerton Youth Theatre for the Lloyds Bank Young Theatre Challenge, 1989, performed at the Royal National Theatre); *Frankie's Monster* (adapted from Vivien Alcock's novel, *The Monster Garden*, Unicorn Theatre, 1991); *Chalk Circle* (Unicorn Theatre, 1991); *Salt of the Earth* (Theatre Centre, 1993); *The Bonekeeper* (Tricycle Youth Theatre, short-listed for the W.H. Smith Awards for plays for children, 1992); *Watch Out for Mr Stork* (one-act play, Soho Theatre Company's Writers' Festival, 1992, and Finborough Theatre, 1995); *Kindertransport* (co-winner of the 1992 Verity Bargate Award, winner of the 1993 Meyer Whitworth Award, performed by Soho Theatre Company, at the Cockpit, 1993, and Manhattan Theater Club, New York, 1994); *Turncoat* (Theatre Centre national tour, 1994); *How to Beat a Giant* (SNAP People's Theatre Trust schools' tour, 1995). Her work for BBC Radio includes: *Whatever Happened to Janet and John/Two Together?* (Radio 4, 1993); *Frankie's Monster* (Radio 5 adaptation of her stage play, 1992); and *Watch Out for Mr Stork* (Radio 4, 1994). Diane Samuels is currently writing *Doctor Y* for the Soho Theatre Company in collaboration with the Royal National Theatre Studio, a radio version of *Kindertransport* and *Swine* for BBC Radio 4; *One Hundred Million Footsteps* for Quicksilver Theatre Company and *Mata Hari: A Private Performance* for Shared Experience.

DIANE SAMUELS

KINDERTRANSPORT

NICK HERN BOOKS
London

A Nick Hern Book

Kindertransport first published in Great Britain in 1995
as a paperback original by Nick Hern Books Limited,
14 Larden Road, London W3 7ST

Passages of German based on a translation by Rena Gamsa.
Personal accounts of the Kindertransport reproduced with
permission

Front cover photo copyright © Hulton Deutsch Collection Ltd.
Collage design copyright © 1995 by Jane Harper

Typeset by Country Setting, Woodchurch, Kent T26 3TB

Printed by Athenæum Press Ltd, Gateshead, Tyne & Wear

A CIP catalogue record for this book is available from the
British Library

ISBN 1 85459 227 0

*Dedicated to all the Jewish 'Kinder' who caught the trains
from Nazi occupied Europe to England in 1938/39,
particularly Walter Fulop, Bertha Leverton, Paula Hill,
Vera Gissing and Lisa who talked at length to me about
their journeys and lives.*

*Many thanks to Libby Mason, Mark Ravenhill, Jack Bradley,
Abigail Morris, and the Cockpit Theatre Workshop programme
for their dramaturgical support. And with special thanks to
Rena Gamsa, Dawn Waterman, Naomi Fulop, Erica Burman,
and particularly to Simon Garfield, B. J. and Jake.*

Author's Note

Three incidents led me to write *Kindertransport*. The first was
a discussion with a close friend, in her late twenties and born
into a comfortable, secure home, who described her struggle to
deal with the guilt of survival. Her father had been on the
Kindertransport and I was struck at how her parent's feelings
had been passed down so fully to her. The second was the
experience of another friend who, at her father's funeral,
overheard her mother recalling her time in Auschwitz. Until
that moment she had had no idea that her mother had been in a
concentration camp. The third was the ashamed admission by a
fifty-five year old woman on a television documentary about
the Kindertransport, that the feeling she felt most strongly
towards her dead parents was rage at their abandonment of her.
What is the cost of survival? What future grows out of a
traumatised past?

Past and present are wound around each other throughout
the play. They are not distinct but inextricably connected. The
re-running of what happened many years ago is not there to
explain how things are now, but is a part of the inner life of the
present.

I interviewed a number of the Kinder as part of my research.
They were all very open about their lives and feelings. Many of
their actual experiences are woven into the fabric of the play.
Although Eva/Evelyn and her life are fictional, most of what
happens to her did happen to someone somewhere.

DIANE SAMUELS

Background to the Kindertransport

The Nazi gaining of power in the 1930's signalled a huge
escalation in anti-semitic activity. The first organised attack on
the Jews was in April 1933 – a boycott of Jewish businesses
was instigated and triggered much violence. A series of laws
ensued, increasingly excluding Jews from public life. The most
notorious of these were the Nuremberg Laws – the Reich
Citizenship Act, depriving Jews of their citizenship, and the
Act for the Protection of German Blood and German Honour.
This latter law prohibited marriage or extramarital relations
between 'Jews and nationals of German or allied blood'
in order to ensure the survival of the German race. Later
measures required that all Jewish passports were marked with
the letter J — in addition Jews were banned from places of
public entertainment and cultural institutions, had their driving
licences revoked, their property confiscated and were often
forced to live together in communal Jewish houses.

The killing of a German diplomat by a young Jew in Paris in
November 1938 gave the Nazis the opportunity to engineer a
huge increase in momentum. Thousands of Jewish businesses
and institutions were destroyed and Jews were assaulted, killed
and 30,000 herded into concentration camps. It was in response
to this pogrom, known as Kristallnacht, that the Movement for
the Care of Children from Germany was formed, rescuing
almost 10,000 unaccompanied children, before the outbreak of
war just nine months later.

Personal Accounts of the Kindertransport

I took a bus to Dovercourt where I was told help was needed at a refugee camp. This was in 1938 when the Committee for the Care of Children from Germany took over a holiday camp to act as a reception centre for Jewish refugee children.

Through this camp came children from Germany, Austria and even a few stray Sudetenlanders. At one time – when I first was there – nearly seven hundred children arrived every week, their passports altered so that all the boys were Jacob and the girls Sarah, carrying pathetic paper bags containing a few spare clothes and little else. The Germans had stripped them of everything that was worth a pfennig. The children had a big J marked on their passports so that everyone would know they were of the despised race. Their ages were at the youngest four and the oldest I remember was sixteen.

The camp was full. As many as came in had to be found places so as to allow room for the next batch. Some children went to relatives in America, many were taken in by families in Britain. Some were even sent to a settlement in Paraguay. Did they, I now wonder, ever come into contact with the Nazis who escaped from Germany and found haven there?

An impressive elderly lady, Anna Essinger – who had a school in Kent – was in charge of the camp and managed, somehow, to shape the ad hoc collection of volunteers into something of an effective organisation. It cannot have been easy: excitable young Viennese, less mercurial German ones, volunteers like myself who arrived by accident and a sprinkling of young Etonians and undergraduates meant there was plenty of energy all needing firm but diplomatic direction.

Dovercourt was important to me if only because it was an introduction to Jewish life. I got to know people there who have remained my friends ever since.

The atmosphere in the camp was highly emotional. The children old enough to understand feared what might be happening to their relatives still in Germany: the refugee staff knew only too well the horrors they had escaped but their friends had not. The whole camp was charged with anxiety and fear. It was there I first heard the word angst and appreciated what it meant.

One evening one of the Austrian volunteers wanted to celebrate a birthday and a half dozen others and myself went to a local hotel for dinner. A change from camp fare where horse meat took the place of beef was something to look forward to. Halfway through the soup, a telephone call came from the camp. A rumour was going round that a pogrom was under way in Vienna: we were needed quickly to help. We rushed back to the camp. It was impossible to describe the situation. Imagine seven hundred contagiously frightened, crying, wailing children milling about the huge and echoing dining hall. The Viennese staff, poor souls, were in almost as bad a state, anguished and caught up in total fear.

We tried to get news of what was happening in Vienna. London apparently knew nothing. Lines to Vienna were blocked as were those to Berlin. Finally we got a contact with Vienna via Czechoslovakia and learned that on that occasion the rumour was false: there was no pogrom.

Then came one of the most moving experiences of my life. It was not going to be easy to stop what had by then become mass hysteria. Shouting above the noise was impossible – if anything it made matters worse. Then one of the older Jewish helpers began to sing. First by himself, a Hebrew hymn which everyone, even the youngest child would know. It was a hymn which I believe had a message of hope and courage in adversity. And the effect gradually spread until within minutes the entire hall was filled with the sound of voices united in song. There was something almost unearthly about such poignant, passionate emotion. Even today, if I ever think of that moment when from wailing the voices changed to singing, my hair stands on end.

The winter of 1938 was a sharp one. At Dovercourt the sea actually froze and when one night high tide and winds combined to break the sea wall, the sea flooded into the camp and we had to carry children through thigh-deep, very cold water to safety. I got pneumonia for my reward and was chased into Dovercourt hospital. After a month or so I returned to the children, who by that time had moved into the old workhouse at Barham near Ipswich, a spooky place complete with cells, mortuary and graveyard.

Shortly after that the war started, no more children came in from the continent and I returned to the land.

HUGH BARRETT
a volunteer at Dovercourt – one of the major
reception centres for the Kindertransport children

Freedom, liberty, human dignity, civil rights, democracy – words and phrases used in the free world to describe the rightful elements of the human condition. If however, in these recessionary times, some if not all of these ideals have a hollow ring, we can at least hope for better days to come. For we may, provided we keep within the law, say and do what we believe to be right and what we believe to be just.

Imagine, however, a society terrorised by a one-party state machinery, where none of this was possible; where the mere label Jew meant the robbing of the individual's humanity and a destiny of extermination.

Faced with this situation, our beloved parents in a spirit of total selfishness chose for us the gift of life, offered by the combined efforts of concerned Jews and Christians, fortunate to be living in the oldest democracy in the world.

Although on arrival, the path for many of us was not exactly strewn with roses, the majority worked hard – grateful for the opportunities denied to the one and a half million children who perished in the holocaust.

Former Kindertransport refugees have made their mark in every sphere of human endeavour. It is salutary to mention that the theatre in which you find yourself tonight was designed by architect Edward Mendelsohn, who came to this country on a Kindertransport in 1939.

PAULA HILL.

The Kindertransport was at the centre of many episodes, which all together added up to one huge destabilising, alienating and ongoing trauma. All Jewish children in Vienna, like myself at the age of ten, were deeply aware of the terror, fear and humiliation which was all around us. And also we continuously heard our parents talking about who had been sent to Buchenwald or Dachau concentration camps; and about trying to get an affidavit from America or a visa to just about anywhere – even to unimaginable Shanghai, if one still had enough money to buy a capitalist visa.

Our family of four had already once escaped to Brussels. We overstayed our three day transit visa limit with disastrous consequences: parents separately arrested; a crack of dawn police swoop; a railway journey to a fictitious refugee camp; the shock of being pushed across the border back into Germany; arrival at Aachen railway station . . . father vanished . . . what to do next? . . . confusion, new shocks and baffling conundrums.

Back in Vienna, confidential, urgent warnings of imminent arrest from a Nazi Party friend forced my father to leave us behind and travel to London by himself, equipped with his two month business visa issued to him for the purpose of registering his photographic patent at the London Patent Office. Staying with a hardworking but poor and newly discovered uncle in the heart of the old London Docks, my father made it his first priority to find a sponsor for me and a live-in housekeeper job for my mother. Uniquely, for such a domestic job, a coveted domestic permit for entry into the country was usually granted.

The actual Kindertransport journey filled me with apprehension as well as anxiety for my mother, who, now all alone, was left behind in hostile Vienna. My brother, at his second attempt, had managed to reach Palestine on a clandestine immigrant ship. Well, in my case my mother did make it to London, to her housekeeper job, before the outbreak of war – in fact by just a few days. And yes, we were all lucky; but everything in life is at a price.

Life with my sponsors, elderly grandparents, themselves immigrants from Bessarabia at the turn of the century, with their totally different background, culture and of course language, had its problems. This episode, followed by evacuation to Wales and Cornwall and life there with Ethel Maude, and her husband Jack-the-Parcel-Office, brought yearnings of reunion with my real parents, who had themselves been forced to live apart.

When such reunion after years of separation finally became possible, my parents had been greatly changed by their experiences and I had been changed beyond recognition by mine. And I was now fifteen years old. Tragically, as a family we were now split in two and decimated. My brother had become rooted in the embryonic Israel. Our relatives had not survived the Holocaust. Most sadly, neither my parents nor myself were able to find in each other the hoped-for image we had built up during our period of separation; and in this way fate robbed us of the pleasure we might otherwise have had in each other. But despite all odds, we had nevertheless survived and it remains a perpetual mystery and wonder how, in the midst of disaster, the seeds of recovery can remain intact.

EDWARD MENDELSOHN.

Travelling to visit my grandparents in Poland as an eight-year-old I found very exciting; snow, droskhas, sledges, halva, but in December 1938 my mother promised me an even greater adventure. I was to be sent to England and, what is more, she said the Queen would be waiting for me with a bunch of flowers on my arrival. At that time, there was little to hold me in Hamburg, when our schooling was virtually ended, our synagogues destroyed and where every shop, cinema, swimming pool, theatre and sweet shop had a notice Jews Unwanted. So, when a group of sad parents gathered at Hamburg Hauptbahnhof to see their children off, the solemnity of the occasion did not strike me. My mother kissed me and left in time to wave me goodbye from the platform as our train passed through the next station, Hamburg-Altona.

I sat in a packed compartment of children of mixed ages. Uniformed men kept entering our compartment, but the journey was uneventful until we crossed the Dutch border when there was singing and jubilation. We were then shepherded aboard a boat at the Hook of Holland bound for Harwich, arriving the following morning. We were shown into a shed, where we were all handed hard-boiled eggs and sandwiches. Some of the older boys prayed – I was ten years old and did not know how to pray, nor quite understand why. I ate my sandwiches and wondered whatever happened to the Queen.

That same night, we were taken to Butlins Holiday Camp in Lowestoft, given two blankets and a wash bowl and shown into a freezing wooden hut with two beds. I was one of about twenty who caught scarlet fever within a week and spent some six weeks in Colchester Isolation Hospital. I was then taken in by a kindly old lady in her guest house for convalescence. It was here, that on my first walk, a lady came up to me and pressed a shilling into my hand.

The ten of us were then taken to a disused Victorian workhouse called Barham House in Claydon, near Ipswich. The house had been converted to house some 800 boys and was just perfect for a ten year old – no discipline, attendance at meals was optional and it was much more fun building a raft and drifting in the nearby river. The house was a selection centre from which boys were sent to adopting parents etc. My turn came at the end of September 1939. I was adopted as a boarder by Oswestry School in Shropshire, a small public school established in 1407. Some of the tradition seemed to have changed little since, but the dormitory was absolute luxury after Barham House. The only problem was I could not speak the language, but I learned English quickly. The school provided humanity in microcosm – there was the bully, the bright, the dull, the strong, the weak. Boys who one moment beat the life out of each other in the playground only minutes later appeared in their white surplices and starched white collars singing and looking like white angels in the school chapel. The culture gap between them and myself was vast, but the gap was bridged and I emerged Head Boy six years later. I left the school feeling very much like any other school leaver, but particularly grateful for my good fortune, the opportunities given to me and the generosity and kindness shown by so many.

In 1949 my good fortune was complete when I was reunited with my parents, who had managed to survive the war by escaping on the last boat out of Europe to Shanghai.

SIGI FAITH

Kinderterror, Kindertransports, Kindertrauma – one sees a
chain of events linking these successive stages in the odyssey
of the children who came in 1938-39. The terror of the children
who, together with their parents, were caught up in a modern
pogrom, Kristallnacht, the night of broken glass and broken
lives, which was the true precursor of the transports. The
transports themselves, that marked the hurriedly and sometimes
frantically arranged wrench, with dimly perceived
consequences, of a child gone from his normal world and
which involved a temporary separation from a family that for
most children would last forever. And then, the trauma of re-
establishing some infrastructure of normality in a strange land,
with new families, however sympathetic and kind, with the
child enjoying a dubious status, neither a temporary guest, nor
adopted, a sort of twilight world of not knowing where he or
she belonged, which was a state of being that was to last, for
some, all their lives.

The personal tragedy of these children has now been
explored and described in numerous accounts, studies, case
histories. But the Kinder also played their part on the much
larger stage of world history. In September 1938, when
Chamberlain returned from Munich waving his bit of paper, he
was undoubtedly greeted by the most rapturous and even
hysterical welcome ever accorded a British prime minister in
any circumstances, let alone one who had just negotiated what
many saw as an ignominious surrender. Less than five and a
half months later, however, the same prime minister was being
pushed by a huge groundswell of public opinion to change his
policy completely and adopt measures that put Britain on a
head-on collision course with Nazi Germany that would
ultimately lead to war. There had in fact been a sea-change in
public opinion. Traditionally, this is attributed to the occupation
of Czechoslovakia on the 15 March 1939. But, by then, the sea-
change had already taken place. What events took place
between 1 October 1938 and 15 March 1939? Only two of any
note: the pogrom of Kristallnacht on 9 and 10 November, and
from 10 December, the arrival of the first of the
Kindertransports, which were to go on for another nine months.

One historian has described the public mood after this as a
reaction to being conned. However dishonourable Munich had

been perceived to be, it was meant to buy settlement, stability and peace. And what it had seemed within weeks to have produced was a pogrom and photographs on newsreels and in newspapers of unaccompanied young children carrying their pathetic suitcases and bundles of belongings, walking down gangplanks at Harwich. The reaction to this of lots of very ordinary people was one of anger and some sort of obstinate determination to bring something which would ultimately develop into the spirit of Dunkirk, Churchill and 1940. It may be some small comfort to those children, more than fifty years on, to know that that, even in some small measure, and quite unwittingly, is what they helped to bring about. But they paid, and in some cases still pay, a price.

FRED BARSCHAK

Despite the fact that I have become completely anglicised, or perhaps because of it, I do not talk readily to people (except very close friends) about my origins. I want to be thought of as completely English. Unfortunately I still cannot knit the English way, and for that reason will never knit in public. I suppose this is because I don't want to be different from real English people. I never think of my birthplace as home now and never refer to it as such.

Extract from We Came as Children, *edited by Karen Gershon and published by Macmillan London Ltd.*

Soho Theatre Company

In 1972 the Soho Theatre Company was established at the Soho
Poly with a mission to produce new plays and discover new
playwrights, among them Caryl Churchill, David Edgar, Barrie
Keeffe, Hanif Kureishi, Pam Gems, Tony Marchant, Sue
Townsend and Timberlake Wertenbaker.

Under the new artistic direction of Abigail Morris, Soho
relaunched the Cockpit Theatre in September 1992, creating
one of the country's largest venues dedicated to new writing.
The opening 13 months saw the presentation of 21 new plays, a
transfer to New York, awards and nominations for Time Out,
the Writers' Guild, the London Fringe, LWT Plays on Stage,
the new Peggy Ramsay Award and the Peter Brook/Empty
Space Award. In July 1995, Soho had to leave the Cockpit, and,
as this book went to press, the Company is actively seeking a
new theatre in central London. The Company's present address
is 24 Mortimer Street, London W1N 7RD.

Meanwhile, Soho Theatre Company's work with writers
continues on a year round basis. From the 1,500 or so scripts
received, read and reported upon each year, some 80 writers are
invited to join the workshop programme. They will become
part of the Research and Development process which is at the
heart of STC's success and makes it unique amongst new
writing theatres.

Built into this programme – workshops, showcase productions,
rehearsed readings, the Verity Bargate Award, commissions
and script surgeries, there is a clear route to production for the
emergent writer of talent.

Diane Samuels' work was discovered by Soho Theatre
Company in 1990. She joined the workshop programme in
1991 and took part in *A Round*, a showcase for short new plays
in the following year. Meanwhile *Kindertransport* was 'work-
shopped' in 1992 and went on to win the Verity Bargate Award

later that year. It was first produced by Soho Theatre Company
at the Cockpit Theatre, London in 1993 and again at Manhattan
Theater Club, New York in 1994.

*'If there is going to be any theatre, apart from musicals, in 20
years' time, the Soho Theatre Company . . . will probably have
been its seed-bed'* The Tatler

Kindertransport was first performed by the Soho Theatre
Company at the Cockpit Theatre, London on 13 April 1993
with the following cast:

RATCATCHER	Nigel Hastings
EVA	Sarah Shanson
HELGA	Ruth Mitchell
EVELYN	Elizabeth Bell
FAITH	Suzan Sylvester
LIL	Doreen Andrew

Directed by Abigail Morris
Designed by Tom Piper
Lighting by Mark Ridler
Music and sound Richard Heacock

Kindertransport was subsequently first performed in the United
States of America by the Manhattan Theater Club at City
Center, Stage 1, New York, in May 1994 with the following
cast:

RATCATCHER	Michael Gaston
EVA	Alanna Ubach
HELGA	Jane Kaczmarek
EVELYN	Dana Ivey
FAITH	Mary Mara
LIL	Patricia Kilgarriff

Directed by Abigail Morris
Scenery by John Lee Beatty
Lighting by Don Holder
Music and sound by Guy Sherman/Aural Fixation

KINDERTRANSPORT

Characters

EVELYN: English middle-class woman. In her fifties.

FAITH: Evelyn's only child. In her early twenties.

EVA: Evelyn's younger self. She starts the play at 9 years old and finishes it at 17 years old. Jewish German becoming increasingly English.

HELGA: German Jewish woman of the late 1930's. In her early thirties. Eva/Evelyn's mother.

LIL: Eva/Evelyn's English foster mother. In her eighties.

THE RATCATCHER: A mythical character who also plays: THE NAZI BORDER OFFICIAL, THE ENGLISH ORGANISER, THE POSTMAN, THE STATION GUARD.

The play takes place in a spare storage room in Evelyn's house in an outer London suburb in recent times.

ACT ONE

Scene One

Pipe music.

Dusty storage room filled with crates, bags, boxes and some old furniture.

EVA, *dressed in clothes of the late thirties, is sitting on the floor, reading. The book is a large, hard-backed children's story book entitled 'Der Rattenfänger'.*

HELGA *enters. She is well turned-out in clothes of the late thirties. She is holding a coat, two buttons, a needle and some thread.*

EVA. What's an abyss, Mutti?

HELGA (*sitting down and ushering* EVA *to sit next to her*). An abyss is a deep and terrible chasm.

EVA. What's a chasm?

HELGA. A huge gash in the rocks.

EVA. What's a . . .

  EVA *puts down the book.*

  Pipe music stops.

HELGA. Eva, sew on your buttons now. Show me that you can do it.

EVA. I can't get the thread through the needle. It's too thick. You do it.

HELGA. Lick the thread . . .

EVA. Do I have to?

HELGA. Yes. Lick the thread.

EVA. I don't want to sew.

HELGA. How else will the buttons get onto the coat?

EVA. The coat's too big for me.

HELGA. It's to last next winter too.

EVA. Please.

HELGA. No.

EVA. Why won't you help?

HELGA. Weren't you old enough to light the candles?

EVA. This is different.

HELGA. You have to be able to manage on your own.

EVA. Why?

HELGA. Because you do. Now, lick the thread.

  EVA *licks the thread.*

HELGA. That should flatten it . . . And hold the needle firmly
  and place the end of the thread between your fingers . . . not
  too near . . . that's it . . . now try to push it through.

  EVA *concentrates on the needle and thread.* HELGA
  watches closely.

HELGA. See. You don't need me. It's good.

EVA. I don't mind having my coat open a bit. Really. I've got
  enough buttons.

HELGA. You'll miss it when the wind blows.

EVA. Can't I do it later?

HELGA. There's no 'later' left, Eva.

EVA. After the packing, after my story . . .

HELGA. Now.

  EVA *gives in and sews.*

  A key jangles in the door lock. It unlocks. The door opens.
  EVELYN *enters. She is carrying a tea towel. She surveys
  the room. If she sees* HELGA *and* EVA, *even momentarily,
  she ignores them. She is followed by* FAITH.

EVELYN. Most of it's junk.

FAITH. You don't keep junk.

EVELYN. Do you want anything in particular?

FAITH. Not really.

EVELYN (*opening a box*). Pans?

FAITH. All those?

EVELYN. Are you intending to cook or eat raw?

FAITH. I was thinking of take-aways . . .

EVELYN. Have them.

> EVELYN *hands the box over to* FAITH *who receives it.*

EVELYN. What else? Lights, crockery, cutlery, there's a
    television somewhere . . .

FAITH. You sound like a shop assistant trying to make a sale.

EVELYN. Just don't be a difficult customer.

FAITH. I wasn't going to be.

EVELYN. Good. I told Mum we wouldn't be long.

> EVELYN *opens a box and takes out a tea cup.*

EVELYN. Would cups and saucers be of any use?

FAITH. I prefer mugs.

EVELYN. What about for visitors?

FAITH. They can have mugs too.

EVELYN. I'll give you this set of cups and saucers just in case.

FAITH. Mum, I . . .

EVELYN. Here's a spare teapot too.

FAITH. I don't really want two teapots.

EVELYN. One might break.

FAITH (*handing the spare one back*). Please keep it.

EVELYN. Must you be so ungrateful?

FAITH. You don't have to do this.

EVELYN. Who else is going to?

FAITH. Dad sent me another cheque.

EVELYN. Would you use a strainer?

FAITH. Not really.

EVELYN. I'm sure his money will come in very useful if you save it.

FAITH. I really wouldn't mind buying my own stuff.

EVELYN. You usually approve of my taste.

FAITH. It's not that.

EVELYN. I'm glad to hear it.

FAITH. You should keep your things.

EVELYN. I don't think I need them as much as you, darling.

FAITH. You might do one day.

EVELYN. They shouldn't be left to moulder in a box when they can be used.

EVELYN *opens a box and takes out a glass. She polishes it.*

EVELYN. Glasses?

FAITH. Those must be worth a fortune.

EVELYN. Nothing is too good for my daughter.

FAITH. They might be too good for the flat.

EVELYN. You said you were very pleased with this one.

FAITH. The rent's so high for what it is.

EVELYN (*polishing*). You said it was a bargain.

FAITH. Maybe you should have come to see it.

EVELYN. You're quite capable of choosing a place to live without my help. You have your friends to advise you.

FAITH. I think they want different things to me.

EVELYN. Isn't it a little late to realise that?

FAITH. Maybe it's not such a good idea to move.

EVELYN *concentrates on polishing and replacing glasses.*

FAITH. I don't feel right about it.

EVELYN *continues to polish. Pause.*

EVELYN (*scrutinising a glass*). This is chipped.

FAITH. What do you think about waiting till I can afford to buy somewhere?

EVELYN. I think that if you say you're going, you should go.

FAITH. I can get the deposit back.

EVELYN. Like you got the deposit back last time?

FAITH. That was different.

EVELYN. It sounds remarkably similar to me.

FAITH. I'm not sure I like it at all, really.

EVELYN. Oh Faith, for heavens sakes, you're impossible.

FAITH. I wish you'd come and see it.

EVELYN (*polishing madly*). How on earth did that glass get damaged? I put in enough paper.

FAITH. I don't like leaving you on your own . . .

EVELYN (*holding open another box*). Tablecloths?

FAITH *shakes her head.* EVELYN *puts them back.*

FAITH. You're angry.

EVELYN. Absolutely not.

FAITH. Are we friends?

EVELYN. Of course.

EVELYN *polishes.*

FAITH. I don't want to go.

EVELYN (*still polishing*). Will eleven glasses be enough?

FAITH. You can forget about the glasses.

EVELYN. You'll need something to drink from in your new home.

EVELYN *continues to polish.* FAITH, *helpless, watches.*

EVA (*sewing*). Why aren't Carla and Heinrich going on one of the trains?

HELGA. Their parents couldn't get them places.

EVA. Carla said it's because they didn't want to send them away.

HELGA. Carla says a lot of silly things.

EVA. Why's that silly?

HELGA. Of course they would send them away if they had places. Any good parent would do that.

EVA. Why?

HELGA. Because any good parent would want to protect their child.

EVA. Can't you and Vati protect me?

HELGA. Only by sending you away.

EVA. Why will I be safer with strangers?

HELGA. Your English family will be kind.

EVA. But they don't know me.

HELGA. Eva. This is for the best.

EVA. Will you miss me?

HELGA. Of course, I will.

EVA. Will you write to me?

HELGA. I've told you. I will do more than miss you and write to you. Vati and I will come. We will not let you leave us behind for very long. Do you think we would really let you go if we thought that we would never see you again?

EVA. How long will it be before you come?

HELGA. Only a month or two. When the silly permits are ready.

EVA. Silly permits.

HELGA. Silly, silly permits.

EVA. The needle's stuck.

HELGA, *with difficulty, pulls the needle through.*

EVA. Finish it off for me.

HELGA (*holding the sewing back to* EVA). No.

EVA *takes it and carries on sewing.*

EVELYN *is still polishing glasses.* FAITH *is still watching her.*

FAITH. Mum, please stop doing that.

EVELYN (*holding up the glass*). They really need washing.

FAITH. This isn't to wind you up, I promise . . .

EVELYN. You can't stay here forever.

FAITH. Do you really want me to go?

EVELYN. What I want is irrelevant.

FAITH. Do you?

EVELYN. This is your life, Faith.

FAITH. It affects you too.

EVELYN. You've made a commitment to moving into that place. Stick by it.

FAITH. It feels all wrong.

EVELYN. It seems perfectly straightforward to me.

FAITH. What do you want?

EVELYN. I want you to make a mature and reliable decision. An adult decision. This continual vacillation is not helpful to either of us.

FAITH. I can't move out yet.

EVELYN *stops polishing.*

EVELYN. Yet?

FAITH. For a while.

EVELYN. What does that mean?

FAITH. Until after I've finished college.

EVELYN. Give it a try at least.

FAITH. I'm not going.

EVELYN. What have you got to lose?

FAITH. I'm definitely staying.

EVELYN. Are you absolutely sure?

FAITH. Absolutely.

EVELYN. So, I can't sell the house?

FAITH. No.

EVELYN. I'll have to phone the estate agent?

FAITH. Yes.

EVELYN. And say no?

FAITH. Yes.

EVELYN. How absurd.

FAITH. I'm sorry.

EVELYN. Are you intending to change your mind again?

FAITH. I don't understand why you have to sell the house if I
    leave . . .

EVELYN. Will you or will you not change your mind?

FAITH. No.

EVELYN. Song and dance finally over?

FAITH. Yes.

   EVELYN *puts back the glass and closes the box.*

EVELYN. I expect you to keep to your word.

   She picks up the chipped glass.

FAITH. Why are you taking that?

EVELYN. A chipped glass is ruined forever.

   EVELYN *exits.* FAITH *retreats back into the attic.*

HELGA. Try to meet other Jews in England.

EVA. I will.

HELGA. They don't mind Jews there. It's like it was here when I was younger. It'll be good.

EVA. When you come, will Vati get his proper job back like he used to have?

HELGA. I'm sure he will.

EVA (*finishes sewing*). Finished.

HELGA. Now let me check the case.

EVA. I packed what you said. It's very full.

HELGA *picks up a case hidden amongst the boxes and opens and checks through it.* EVA *watches her.*

FAITH *finds a trunk. She is tempted to look inside. She hesitates. She takes courage and tentatively opens it.*

HELGA (*pulling out a dress*). This suits you so well.

EVA. I'll only wear it for best. Promise.

HELGA (*re-folding the dress*). Someone will have to press out the creases when you get there.

FAITH (*pulling out a toy train*). Runaway train?

EVA. Did I fold it wrongly?

HELGA. No. The case is far too small.

FAITH *makes the sound of a train whistle as she pulls pieces of train track out of the box. She starts to lay them out on the floor.*

FAITH. Runaway train went down the track
And she blew, she blew
Runaway train went down the track
And she blew, she blew
Runaway train went down the track
And blah de blah, she won't come back
And she blew, blew, blew, blew
Blew!

FAITH *continues to lay the track.*

HELGA *pulls a mouth organ out of the case.*

HELGA. What's this doing in here?

EVA. That's my mouth organ.

HELGA. You're not allowed to take anything other than clothes.

EVA. But it was my last birthday present and I'm just beginning to get the tunes right.

HELGA. The border guards will send you back to us if they find you with this. Then where will you be?

EVA. I'm sorry.

HELGA gives the mouth organ to EVA and sets to reorganising the case contents.

FAITH looks into another box. She turns it upside down. A load of dolls fall on to the floor. None of them have any clothes on.

FAITH. Jesus. She's got all my dolls. Where are the clothes?

FAITH picks up a doll.

Lucy?

She gently sits Lucy by the train set.

FAITH picks out another doll.

Gloria.

She gently sits Gloria next to Lucy and then does the same with each of the other dolls.

HELGA. There's no room for anything else. Where are your shoes?

EVA reaches over to right by FAITH's feet and gets a pair of shoes.

FAITH (*laying out another doll*). Barbara.

FAITH continues to lay out the dolls.

EVA. Here.

HELGA. Put the heel of the right shoe to your ear.

EVA. Why?

HELGA. Do it.

EVA puts the heel to her ear.

HELGA. What can you hear?

EVA. It sounds like . . .

HELGA. Yes?

EVA. Ticking.

HELGA. My gold watch is in there.

EVA. How?

HELGA. The cobbler did it.

EVA. I'll look after it for you.

HELGA. And in the other heel are two rings, a chain with a
    Star of David and a charm bracelet for you. All made of
    gold.

EVA. For me?

HELGA. From my jewellery box. A travelling gift.

EVA. Thank you.

HELGA. My grandfather used to wear a black hat and coat.
    'You are my children. You are my jewels.' He told me. 'We
    old ones invest our future in you.'

    EVA *hugs* HELGA.

    LIL *enters.*

LIL. You two have the quietest arguments.

FAITH. Is she still not pleased?

LIL. So so.

FAITH. You think it's better if I stay, don't you?

LIL. Doesn't bother me either way.

FAITH. But don't you . . . ?

LIL. I'm keeping out of it.

FAITH. Sorry, Gran.

LIL. What for?

FAITH. Spoiling the start of your visit.

LIL. I've seen worse.

FAITH. Where is she now?

LIL. Cleaning the windows. She's begun in the sitting room.

FAITH. The cleaner came yesterday.

LIL. She's even got the step ladder out.

FAITH. What about the pink overall?

LIL. Oh yes.

FAITH. Oh god.

LIL. She'll sparkle the glass and then it'll be done.

FAITH. Is she talking?

LIL. Lock jaw's set in.

FAITH. Don't you just love it?

LIL. Coming down?

FAITH (*looking at the toys*). I found some of my old things. I'd no idea she'd kept them.

LIL. You've made a mess, haven't you?

FAITH. Only laying them out.

LIL. You'll make your mum even worse.

FAITH. What's wrong with looking at my old toys?

LIL. Is she cleaning her guts out downstairs for you to wreak havoc in her precious attic?

FAITH. Gran, there's no harm meant.

LIL. There's harm caused.

FAITH. I'll pack them up before she comes in here again.

LIL. You're trying to set her off on purpose aren't you?

FAITH. No.

LIL. Well, stop being soft and put them away now.

FAITH. Why is it that I can't do a simple, ordinary thing without getting it in the neck?

LIL. Since when have you done things simply where she's concerned?

FAITH. Believe me, I hate it when she gets like this.

LIL. You could do a much better job of keeping her sweet then.

FAITH. Story of my life.

LIL. Just get this lot boxed and neaten up the room. I'll do tea.

LIL *exits.*

FAITH *reluctantly starts put the dolls back into the box.*

HELGA *and* EVA *break their embrace.*

EVA. Listen.

HELGA. What?

EVA. I've nearly got it right.

EVA *starts to play a tune on the mouth organ. She plays well.*

EVA *finishes playing.* HELGA *applauds.*

FAITH *pulls out small box. She opens and looks inside.*

HELGA. Now it's time for bed.

EVA. Not yet. Let me stay up. It's my last night.

HELGA. We will carry on as we always do. Bedtime is bedtime.

EVA (*moaning*). Mutti.

HELGA. Which story do you want?

HELGA *turns and picks up* EVA*'s 'Rattenfänger' book.*

EVA *quickly sneaks her mouth organ into the case and closes it.*

EVA. The Ratcatcher.

FAITH *pulls out a hard-backed children's story book identical to the one* HELGA *is holding.*

Pipe music.

FAITH. 'Der Rattenfänger'.

HELGA. Not that one, Eva.

EVA. You said I could choose.

HELGA. Choose something else.

EVA. I don't want anything else.

HELGA *opens the book and turns its pages.*

FAITH. The Ratcatcher?

EVA. What did you say an abyss was, Mutti?

HELGA. I hope you won't ask questions like this when you're in England.

EVA. Why not?

HELGA. Listen.

FAITH *opens the book and flicks through it. She finds an inscription in the front of the book.*

EVA *sits close to* HELGA.

HELGA. Beware little children. Beware and take heed. Learn the lesson of Hamlyn where one bad soul brought tragedy upon the whole town.

FAITH. Hamburg. 1939.

HELGA. Happy Hamlyn after the rats had been led away . . .

FAITH *carefully looks at the first page.*

HELGA. . . . A town teeming with life. Full to overflowing. And every day, the good people counted their blessings. Every single one . . . Eva?

EVA. I'm listening.

FAITH (*looking at a picture*). Counting their blessings for being so lucky . . .

HELGA. They all knew how fortunate they were. All except for one very wicked soul who was ungrateful and did not count.

FAITH (*looking at another picture*). Mr Ingratitude. Jesus.

HELGA. 'We are forgotten. We are lost . . .

EVA. . . . We are destroyed . . . '

HELGA. . . . cried out all the uncounted blessings.

FAITH. The cloud . . .

HELGA. Then a cloud appeared in the clear, blue sky casting a shadow down below.

EVA. Who is not counting?

HELGA. Whispered the shadow.

EVA. Who has forgotten their blessings?

HELGA. It hissed.

EVA. I will find you.

HELGA. It spat.

EVA. I will search you out whoever wherever you are.

FAITH (*turning onto another page*). My god, and the shadow growing legs . . .

HELGA. ' . . . and strong arms and spiky nails . . . '

EVA. And eyes sharp as razors.

FAITH. The Ratcatcher.

The shadow of the RATCATCHER *hovers.*

A train whistle blows. Sounds of a busy railway station.

HELGA *remains stuck in bedtime story mode.* EVA *puts on her coat and hat and label with her number on it – 3362.*

HELGA. The Ratcatcher searched for the ungrateful one. He searched and searched but all in vain.

RATCATCHER. Who is to pay for the lost blessings?

HELGA. He raged.

RATCATCHER. If not the one guilty soul, then all.

HELGA. And he raised an enchanted pipe to his snarling lip, making a cruel promise to all the people of Hamlyn.

RATCATCHER. I will take the heart of your happiness away.

The RATCATCHER *plays his music.*

The sounds of the railway station become louder and louder.

Another train whistle.

EVA. Mutti! Vati! Hello! Hello! See. I did get into the carriage.
I said I would. See, I'm not crying. I said I wouldn't. I can't
open the window! It's sealed tight! Why've you taken your
gloves off? You're knocking too hard. Your knuckles are
going red! What? I can't hear you!

Sound of long, shrill train whistle.

EVA. Louder! Louder! What! I can't hear! I can't . . . See you
in England.

Sounds of train starting to move. EVA *sits.*

EVA. I mustn't stare at that cross-eyed boy.

Train whistle blows.

EVA. What if he talks to me?

*Sounds of children chattering. Suddenly a young child cries
and cries.*

EVA. You mustn't cry. There's no point.

The crying continues.

EVA. Stop it.

The crying continues.

EVA. We'll all see our muttis and vatis soon enough.

The crying calms slightly.

EVA. And don't look at that cross-eyed boy.

The crying continues.

EVA. Hoppe, hoppe Reiter / Wenn er fällt dann schreit er / Fällt
er in den Graben / Fressen ihn die Raben / Fällt er in den
Sumpf / Macht der Reiter plumpf. (Hop hop hop hop rider /
Do not fall beside her / If into the ditch you fall / The
Ratman gets you all / And don't have the desire / To fall into
the mire.)

The crying calms. Sounds of children laughing.

EVA (*announcing to all around her*). Did any of you know? In
England all the men have pipes and look like Sherlock
Holmes and everyone has a dog.

Enter a Nazi BORDER OFFICIAL. *He approaches* EVA.

FAITH *watches.*

OFFICIAL. No councillor in here?

EVA. She's in the next carriage.

OFFICIAL *(picking up* EVA*'s case).* Whose case is this?

EVA. Mine.

OFFICIAL. Stand up straight.

EVA *stands.*

OFFICIAL. Turn your label round then. It's gone the wrong way. Can't see your number.

EVA *(turning the label round. Quietly).* Sorry.

OFFICIAL. Speak up.

EVA. Sorry.

OFFICIAL. Sir! Sorry, Sir.

EVA. Sorry, Sir.

OFFICIAL. No one will know what to do with you if they can't see your number.

Silence.

Will they?

EVA. No, Sir.

OFFICIAL. Might have to remove you from the train.

Silence.

Mightn't we?

EVA. Yes, Sir.

OFFICIAL. D'you know it at least?

EVA. Pardon, Sir?

OFFICIAL. Know your number. If you don't know it you might forget who you are.

EVA. 3362, Sir.

OFFICIAL (*taking out a pen*). Don't want you to forget who you are now, do we?

EVA. No, Sir.

OFFICIAL. Let me remind you.

He draws a huge Star of David on the label.

OFFICIAL. There. That should tell 'em wherever it is you're going. Best to keep them informed, eh?

EVA (*terrified*). Yes, Sir.

OFFICIAL *opens and searches the case, throwing everything onto the floor. He finds the mouth organ.*

OFFICIAL. You can't take valuables out of the country. Can't take anything for gain.

EVA. I wouldn't sell it, Sir.

OFFICIAL. What's it for then?

EVA. For music, Sir. I play it, Sir.

OFFICIAL. You any good?

EVA. I suppose so . . .

OFFICIAL. Go on then. Prove it's not just to make money.

EVA *takes it and plays nervously, badly.*

OFFICIAL. You need more practice. Better keep it.

OFFICIAL *body searches EVA.*

OFFICIAL. What money have you got?

OFFICIAL *digs into EVA's pockets and takes out a few coins which he takes and pockets.*

OFFICIAL. Better clear up the mess.

EVA *starts to clear up.*

OFFICIAL *feels in a pocket and produces a toffee.*

OFFICIAL (*giving the toffee to EVA*). Here kiddie. A sweetie for you.

OFFICIAL *ruffles EVA's hair and exits.*

EVA *grips the toffee tightly and tidies up the clothes into the case.*

Sounds of a train speeding along. Children's excited chatter. In German, 'Es ist die Grenze, die Grenze, die Grenze' ('The border, the border, the border').

EVA. It is the border! The border! Can't get us now! We're out! Out! Stuff your stupid Hitler. Stuff your stupid toffees! (*She throws down the toffee.*) Keep them! Hope your eyes fall out and you die the worst death on earth! Hope you all rot in hell for ever and ever! Hope no one buries you! Hope the rats come and eat up all your remains until there's nothing left!

Sounds of a train stopping. Sounds of a buzzing, busy happy crowd at a railway station. A voice saying in Dutch, 'Have as many sweets and as much lemonade as you want.'

EVA (*greedily eating and drinking*). You know what? That Dutch lady said we can have as many cakes as we want. And sweets. And lemonade. I'm going to stuff my pockets for later. Who says it's naughty? They all want us to be happy, don't they? Well, that's what I'm doing. Making myself happy.

Sound of a ship's horn and the lapping of waves. Tired, muted children's chatter.

EVA. You know what? If you lick your lips you'll taste the salt. Sea salt. What d'you mean, Hook of Holland? It can't be. It's nothing like one. It isn't. Look at it. How's that a hook? (*Coughing.*). Excuse me . . . (*About to vomit.*) . . . it won't come . . . No, I'm fine . . . Really . . . It's just nothing . . . Nothing will come out of me.

Sound of a ship's horn.

EVA. This is Harwich, you know. It really is England.

Sounds of disembarkation. Children's chatter and adult English voices, 'Come along now', 'Keep moving', 'Move to the right, please'.

EVA. Can you just go through like that? Don't they search you?

EVA *stops and bends down suddenly.*

EVA (*picking up one penny*). A penny. They have big money here. It must be a sign of good luck.

EVA *pockets the penny.*

Ratcatcher's music.

HELGA. In the piper's wake they skipped. All the children up the mountain, on and on till . . . crash. With a roar the rock opened, the music stopped, and the children disappeared into the abyss.

FAITH (*reading*). Strasse der Unverführbarkeit. ('Drumless Street'.)

HELGA. And the weeping people renamed the street where the children had last been seen, 'Drumless Street'. A hollow highway where music was forbidden. Then chisel and hammer battered into the walls of Hamlyn the tragic tale of the lost kinder who left in the summer of 1284 and were never seen thereafter.

FAITH *starts to play a discordant tune on the mouth organ.*

Blackout.

Scene Two

HELGA *has gone.*

FAITH *has settled down to read a letter from the box.*

EVA *has taken her coat off. Her case is by her feet. She has a tin mug of tea in one hand and a piece of bread in the other.*

Railway station sounds. A train announcement in English.

EVA (*trying to put on a brave face*). I am very lucky. I appreciate all of this, really I do, Mutti.

She takes a bite out of the bread.

FAITH (*reading*). March 6th, 1941.

EVA. I'm glad to be eating the bread of freedom even if it does taste like sponge buttered with greasy salt.

She sips the tea.

FAITH. 'Dearest Eva, little Eva who must now be so big.'

EVA. How good it is to sip the tea of England even if it does taste like dishwater. I am so fortunate not to be at home with you and Vati. How good it is to have escaped.

FAITH. See, I write you in English for sure am I that it now is your best language.

EVA. If I could, if it wasn't ungrateful, I'd wish that they hadn't made this 'stuff' for me so I had to drink and eat it; wish that the houses I saw on the way here weren't all the same, red-brick squares so I could look forward to living somewhere like our house, elegant; wish they all spoke German.

EVA *sighs and takes another sip.*

FAITH. Tantchen Marianne send her love. She is not too well at present as her chest is very bad. It does not help that we have poor heating here in the small flat that Vati and me now share with her.

EVA. Mind you, Mutti, it was wonderful going on the red bus. We went right through London. I sat on the top. I could see everything. Upstairs on a bus. It's unbelievable!

FAITH. Are you keeping up your good studies at school and working as hard and well as always you did? Also we hope that you be a good girl for the Mr and Mrs Miller. Vati wants me to tell you that he is well and his spirits are up. Life is not so bad. We are happy enough.

An English ORGANISER *enters.*

EVA (*standing up and bowing. Very carefully pronouncing*). Good bye to you.

ORGANISER. What you on about?

EVA. About?

ORGANISER. Never mind. Is your name Eva (*Pauses to work out the pronunciation.*) Schlesinger?

EVA *looks uncertain.*

ORGANISER. How d'you say it? EEvaa Shshlezzinnjerr?

EVA (*different pronunciation*). Ava Schlesinger?

ORGANISER. Yes. (*Points at her.*) You?

EVA. Schlesinger Eva.

ORGANISER. You are she?

EVA. Ich? (Me?)

ORGANISER. Eva?

EVA. Ja, mein Herr. (Yes, sir.)

ORGANISER. It appears that your English family have been delayed.

EVA. Das verstehe ich nicht. (I don't understand.)

ORGANISER (*miming with hands and talking very slowly*). Your . . . English Mother . . . Mutter?

EVA. Mutter.

ORGANISER (*miming graphically*). Not coming yet!

EVA. Keiner kommt mich abholen? (No one's coming to meet me?)

ORGANISER (*nodding*). That's right.

EVA. Gar keiner? (No one at all?)

ORGANISER (*nodding*). That's right.

EVA. Meine Mutter hat aber gesagt, dass hier eine Familie für mich ist. Sie hat gesagt, das ist alles besprochen. (But my mother said that I had a family here. She said it had been arranged.)

EVA *starts crying.*

ORGANISER. What is it about me that gets them all crying?

EVA. Ich will meine Eltern haben. (I want my parents.)

ORGANISER. I'm sorry, love. I can't understand a word you're saying.

EVA. Und wer wird kümmert sich um mich? (Who will look after me?)

ORGANISER. She'll be here soon.

EVA. Wo soll ich denn hin? (Where will I go?)

ORGANISER. You've just got to wait.

EVA. Bitte, schicken Sie mich nicht zurück nach Deutschland. (Please don't send me back to Germany.)

ORGANISER. It's not the end of the world.

EVA *sniffs.*

ORGANISER (*taking a hankie out of his pocket*). Here.

EVA *hesitates.*

ORGANISER. I've not used it.

EVA *takes it, wipes her eyes and blows her nose.*

ORGANISER. I should really leave you to use your sleeve like most of the others are doing.

EVA (*holding out the hankie to return it*). Entschuldigung, ich habe es ein bisschen schmutzig gemacht. (I'm sorry. I've made it a bit dirty.)

ORGANISER (*taking the hankie*). I just can't stand it when you all start crying.

EVA. Kümmern Sie sich um mich? (Will you look after me?)

ORGANISER. At least you've stopped now. Right. I'd better go and do that lot over there.

ORGANISER *makes to exit.* EVA *makes to follow him.*

ORGANISER. No. No. You stay where you are.

EVA *looks perplexed.*

ORGANISER. (*barking at her as if to a dog*). Sit!

EVA *looks at the chair and returns to it.*

ORGANISER. Stay!

ORGANISER *exits.*

FAITH (*still reading*). Remember that we always love and think of you. Always. No matter what. Mutti.

FAITH starts to play the mouth organ.

EVA (*listening to the heel of her shoe*). Yes. It is. It's ticking.

She tries to twist the heel.

EVA. I need to know the time. Come on.

She twists again with much more effort. Nothing shifts. She holds the heel to her ear and shakes it.

My gold rings. I want to try on my new rings.

She takes off the other shoe.

My chain. I can wear it now. For the first time I can wear it out on top of my clothes.

She thwacks the heels against the side of the chair.

EVA. Mutti, you were right about Herr Reichman. He is a very reliable cobbler who doesn't know how to make a faulty shoe. He's locked in my keepsakes, the gold presents from you and Vati. I'll never get them now. (*Putting the shoe back on.*) They'll just be there in my shoes, jangling and ticking away, with me walking on them for ever and ever. What good's a watch when you can't see its face?

LIL enters.

FAITH. I will put the things away . . .

LIL. You said that before.

FAITH. I'm just about to.

LIL. What about tea?

FAITH. I don't want any.

EVA (*standing up*). Goodbye to you.

LIL (*to EVA*). Poor lamb. You must be exhausted. Scared as well probably. Last thing you need is me being late.

EVA stands and bows.

EVA. Goodbye to you.

LIL. Goodbye?

EVA. Goodbye.

LIL. Who taught you English? German teacher was it? (*Holds out her hand.*). Hello.

EVA *holds out her hand.*

LIL (*shaking* EVA's *hand*). Hello.

EVA (*carefully*). Hello.

LIL (*speaking slowly*). My name is Mrs Miller. Lil Miller.

EVA. Sehr erfreut. (I'm pleased to meet you.)

LIL. I'm sorry, love. Don't speak German. You'll have to learn English.

Points to EVA's *case and gestures 'out'.*

Set to go then?

EVA *picks up her case, puts on her coat and stands ready.*

LIL (*pointing at the label with the number and Star of David on it*). What's this?

EVA. Ach, das ist blöd. (I hate it.)

LIL. Why don't we get rid of it?

EVA *hesitates.*

LIL. You don't need it on now I've come.

EVA. Und wenn ich meine Nummer vergesse? (What if I forget my number?)

LIL *takes the label off.*

LIL. All gone.

LIL *puts the label on the chair.*

EVA. Ist das denn wirklich erlaubt? (Are you sure that you can do that?)

LIL (*gesturing*). Over. Finished. Done. Goodbye. Yes. That's the word. Goodbye.

EVA. Ach so. (I understand.)

LIL *takes her hand.*

LIL. I like you. Come on. D'you like singing?

LIL *sings a snatch of 'Runaway Train'.*

Train to Manchester. Our carriage is served. Sit down there. And don't put your feet on the seats. Doing alright?

LIL *takes out a packet of cigarettes and starts to light up.*

EVA *looks horrified.*

EVA. Weshalb rauchen Sie denn? Sowas tut man doch nicht. (You can't smoke. It's a dirty habit.)

LIL. Don't you like smoking?

EVA. Nur primitive Menschen rauchen. (Only common people smoke.)

LIL. You'll just have to get used to it.

EVA. Davon werden die Finger gelb, wie 'ne Totenhand. (It makes your fingers go yellow and boney.)

LIL. What you on about? Look. (*She takes out a cigarette.*) This is a cigarette. I light it (*She lights it.*) I smoke it. (*She takes a drag.*) Oh, that's good. And I enjoy it. You'll have to learn to go down the shops and get my twenty Players for me. That can be the first English you learn.

EVA (*pointing at the match box and miming striking a match*). Darf ich eine anzünden? (Can I light one?)

LIL. These matches are dangerous, you know. Dangerous. You'll burn yourself.

EVA. Bei meiner Mutter darf ich Streichhölzer benutzen. (My mother lets me use matches.)

LIL. I suppose I've got my eye on you.

LIL *hands her the box.* EVA *strikes the match and lights* LIL*'s cigarette.*

EVA (*pointing at the cigarette*). Kann ich mal probieren? (Can I have a go?)

LIL. Didn't your mam ever tell you that's it's bad for children to smoke?

EVA. Ach, bitte. (Please.)

LIL. You're a naughty girl, you.

EVA. Nur ein einziges Mal. (Just one try.)

LIL (*holding the cigarette out to her*). A quickie then.

EVA *draws on the cigarette and coughs.*

LIL. Away from home, out in the world two minutes and already you're smoking like a chimney.

EVA. I have hunger.

LIL. Should have said before. (*Looking at her watch.*) Five minutes. Alright. Wait there!

LIL *rushes off.*

EVA. Frau Lil! Frau Lil! Lassen Sie mich nich allein! Womöglich fährt der Zug ab! Ich habe nicht mal eine Fahrkarte! Bitte bleiben Sie hier! Wo sind Sie denn! Ich weiss ja nicht, wie ich mit jemandem reden soll. Was soll ich denn machen! (Frau Lil! Frau Lil! Don't leave me! The train might go! I don't even have my ticket! Please come back! (*Looks.*) Where are you! I don't know how to talk to anyone. What'll I do!)

The whistle blows.

EVA. Hilfe! Hilfe! (Help! Help!)

LIL *rushes in holding large piece of cake.*

LIL. Stop fretting and eat your Madeira cake.

She gives the cake to EVA *who eats it hungrily.*

FAITH. I don't want any tea.

LIL. Don't make me have it on my own.

FAITH. What about Mum?

LIL. She's polishing furniture.

FAITH. Has she had the vacuum out yet?

LIL. Stop it.

FAITH. I'm sorry. I'm not hungry.

LIL (*signalling at the mess*). Get on with it, Faith.

FAITH. Gran . . .

LIL. Now.

FAITH. If you don't mind, I'm just looking . . .

LIL (*bending down to pick things up*). Time to come out and face the music, Princess Hideaway.

FAITH. Don't call me that.

LIL. Don't do it then.

FAITH. Look what I've found . . .

FAITH *pulls out Der Rattenfänger book.*

LIL. Stop poking around, will you.

FAITH. It's the Ratcatcher story. I didn't know we had a copy.

LIL. What Ratcatcher story?

FAITH. You know, 'The Ratcatcher ever-ready in the shadows'.

LIL. Don't recall it.

FAITH. Yes you do. All the parents say, 'If you're not good the Ratcatcher will come and get you.' But the children don't listen. And he comes out of the dark night with his spiky nails and razor eyes and tempts them with sweets. And they're so naughty that they follow him into the abyss.

LIL. Why d'you think I know it?

FAITH. Mum used to tell me. She said she was told it when she was little.

LIL. She must have read it herself.

FAITH. She can't have done. Not from this book. It's in German.

LIL. Let me see.

LIL *takes the book and opens it.*

Where did you get this?

FAITH. That box.

LIL *looks in the box at the letters and photos.*

FAITH. Did it belong to the little Jewish girl you had staying with you during the war?

LIL. What d'you mean?

FAITH *picks up a photo and shows it to* LIL.

FAITH. Eva something.

LIL. I see.

FAITH. I read some stuff.

LIL. What have you read?

FAITH. Letters from her parents, bits from her diary . . .

LIL. You should leave things alone.

FAITH. D'you know why Mum's got all her belongings?

LIL. No idea.

FAITH. I'm surprised you've never mentioned her.

LIL. A million things happened during the war.

FAITH. Were you close?

LIL. She wasn't with us for long.

FAITH. It must have been for at least two years . . .

LIL. Was it?

FAITH. Why are you being so cagey?

LIL. I'm hungry for my tea.

FAITH (*joking*). Did you kill her and try to hide the evidence?

LIL. Don't be so bloody stupid!

FAITH. Gran?

LIL. I didn't think that your mother had kept anything from that time.

FAITH. It's upset you, hasn't it?

LIL. I don't know why.

FAITH. Did something bad happen to her?

LIL. To who?

FAITH (*holding up the photo*). Little Eva.

LIL. No. No. She's alright.

FAITH. D'you know where she is?

LIL. Stop going on at me will you.

FAITH. It's OK. Sorry. Don't worry. I'll ask Mum.

LIL. No. Don't. Don't you dare.

FAITH. Why not?

LIL. Just leave it.

FAITH. Why?

LIL *is silent.*

FAITH. What?

LIL *holds out her hand for the photo.*

FAITH *pulls back and looks at the photo closely.*

LIL. Those are your mother's private possessions, Faith.

LIL *holds out her hand for the photo again.*

FAITH *keeps hold.*

FAITH. No they're not. They really belong to that Eva.

LIL *keeps holding out her hand.*

LIL. Your mother's things.

FAITH. Who is this little girl?

LIL. Faith.

FAITH. Who?

LIL *looks down.*

FAITH. Is she something to do with Mum?

LIL *looks down.*

FAITH. Is she Mum?

LIL. Faith.

FAITH. Is she?

LIL. You shouldn't have looked at them.

FAITH. Shit.

LIL. Put them away now.

FAITH. You told me she was three days old when she came to you.

LIL. What am I meant to say?

FAITH. Just answer.

LIL. She was nine years when she came.

FAITH. And she was called Eva?

LIL. I'm not going to lie.

FAITH. And she spoke German and wore a yellow star?

LIL. There was no yellow star.

FAITH. But she was Jewish?

LIL. It was a long time ago.

FAITH. This is unbelievable.

LIL. You really shouldn't have looked.

FAITH. I've asked you both so many times about her real family.

LIL. Aren't I real now?

FAITH. Did you ever meet her parents?

LIL. No.

FAITH. Do you know what happened to them?

LIL. They died.

FAITH. Why make a secret out of it?

LIL. She just wanted to put the past behind her. It was for the best.

FAITH. Whose best?

LIL. Hers.

FAITH. What about mine?

LIL. Don't be so bloody selfish.

FAITH. Don't you think that this affects me?

LIL. It affects her more.

FAITH. I know nothing about her.

LIL. She's still your mam, Faith. Don't make a big deal out of something that was over and done with before you were born.

FAITH. What was the point in having me if she was going to cut herself off?

EVA, *pen and paper in hand, sits on the other side of* LIL.

EVA (*showing the letter to* LIL). My letter is finished.

LIL. Is it now?

EVA. At the hour of lunch I did it. I have help from teacher. She said it to be in mine words. She put some English in.

LIL. Show me.

EVA *gives the letter to* LIL.

LIL (*reading the letter out loud*). 'Sirs, I am nine years old and now have come to live my days in Manchester with a very kind lady and her family by the name of Miller.'

EVA (*taking over the reading*). 'My Mother and Father, Helga and Werner Schlesinger, are not come with me because they would be illegal to do so. But I am much sad that they must to be in Hamburg in Germany because there are dangers in that place for them in that they are Jewish people.' It is in your powers to give them permit that they come into England. Please will you give it to them. Job will be here for them I make sure of it. I remain yours faithfully, Eva Schlesinger.'

LIL. This is good. You write English better than our Nora and she's been speaking it all her life.

EVA. I did all the lunchtime.

LIL. What about your sandwiches? When did you eat them if you were writing all lunchtime?

EVA. Sandwiches got ham in. I not to eat ham. It from pig.

LIL. But I asked you and you said yes.

EVA. Then I think good to eat it looked.

LIL. It is good. Special treat for us all.

EVA. But Mutti I think see me and not be pleased. So not eat. God not like. This is law of Jews.

LIL. Look, love, if it's God you're worried about, the Lord Jesus said that we needn't keep to the old laws any more. They had their day years ago.

EVA. Did they?

LIL. Course they did. Made for olden times. New things have come to put in their place.

EVA. For all persons? Even Jews?

LIL. Especially for Jews.

EVA. Why not all Jews think that?

LIL. Hanging on to the past, I suppose. Now, listen you. Always make time to eat. Always. It matters. There's enough starving children in the world without adding to their number.

EVA. Sorry.

LIL. Well, what will you do tomorrow?

EVA. I eat lunch.

LIL. Else we'll have to call you Skin and Bones . . .

EVA. Please. You do letter.

LIL. Got a lot to do before I can do that. Need to find them jobs. Sort out sponsors. We'll put an ad in the paper. (*Picking up a newspaper.*) Here's the sort of thing. (*Reading.*) 'Married couple, still in Vienna; speak excellent English; want position. Wife perfect cook; husband experienced driver. Write to etc . . . ' Got to word it right.

EVA. Vati is in bank. We write he to be in bank.

LIL. Can't do that love.

EVA. But he do that. He master in bank. Nazis stop him. Here he do again. No Nazis here.

LIL. The only jobs they'll let them do is as servants. I checked. What about gardener?

EVA. Father? No. At home, Herr Kuttel gardener.

LIL. Well, what about cook then?

EVA. Mutti know to cook, I think.

LIL. Cook. Good. And we'll say she can clean. Plus their English is fluent. What about your dad as a butler?

EVA. They not servants!

LIL. Do you want them here as servants or over there?

EVA. If not do servant, they not come?

LIL. No. simple as that.

EVA. Alright. Father could do butler.

LIL. Used to be a bank manager didn't he? Stand the same way do butlers and bank managers.

EVA. Stand same way?

LIL. Like this.

LIL *stands in formal, stiff, straight-backed pose.*

LIL. Butler (*She poses.*) Bank manager (*She poses.*).Same thing.

EVA. Not in Germany.

LIL. Different sense of humour too.

EVA. Sense . . .

LIL. Jokes, lovie. Just jokes.

EVA. We call you Laugh A Minute.

LIL (*chuffed and taken aback*). Where d'you learn that?

EVA. Please do ad now.

LIL (*reading paper*). 'Married couple. Non-Aryan. Very cultured.' We'll copy this.

EVA *takes paper off her and pores over it.*

FAITH (*looking at a photo*). She must have changed a lot.

LIL. She had to cope with a lot.

FAITH. What exactly?

LIL. Losing her parents like that.

FAITH. Like what?

LIL. Coming over on her own . . .

FAITH. Why on her own?

LIL. They only had children on those trains.

FAITH. Why did you take her?

LIL. I wanted to help.

FAITH. But when . . . ?

LIL. You mustn't tell your mother I told you . . .

FAITH. When exactly did she come?

LIL. She arrived on January 7th, 1939.

FAITH. On her birthday.

LIL. It wasn't her birthday then.

FAITH. What d'you mean?

LIL. She changed her birthday. When she was sixteen. She changed it to the day I first picked her up from the station. Promise me you won't tell her, Faith.

FAITH. When's her real birthday?

LIL. Can't recall.

FAITH. But January 7th is on her passport. How could she get away with that?

LIL. She made sure it went onto all the naturalisation papers. She said they'd made a mistake on the papers she came in on.

FAITH. Is that when she changed her name too?

LIL. Yes.

FAITH. Why?

LIL. She just wanted to make a fresh start.

FAITH. So what else did she change?

EVA *sneaks in front of them, trying not to be seen by* LIL.

LIL (*angry*). You're in then. At last. Good. We have to have a talk, young lady.

EVA *goes very quiet. Her head droops.*

LIL. You talk first.

EVA. About what?

LIL. Lying.

EVA. I not know . . .

LIL. Yes you do. Where have you been?

EVA. Alles hängt nur von mir ab. Ich muss einfach. (It's all up to me. I have to.)

LIL. Not the German, Eva.

EVA. Ich muss sie befreien. Ausser mir . . . ist keiner . . . da. (I have to get them out. There's no one else.)

LIL. Don't hide behind the German. It won't protect you and you know it.

EVA. Sie dürfen mich aber nicht daran hindern. (You mustn't try to stop me.)

LIL. In English! English!

EVA. Nicht Englisch! Deutsch! Ich bin Deutsche! (Not English! German! I'm German!)

LIL. I've had enough of this, you little snake! Bloody stop it!

EVA (*sobbing*). No good. No good.

LIL. Cut out the snivels! Now! I want facts from you! True ones! Where've you been!

EVA. English lesson.

LIL. How long for?

EVA. Two hours.

LIL. It's half past six now.

EVA. Walk home slow.

LIL. You're not learning English.

EVA. You not like . . .

LIL. If there's one thing I cannot stand, it's a little liar!
    Where've you been!

EVA. Please . . .

LIL. Now! Before I chuck you out and never let you back in!

EVA. I can't.

LIL. You bloody well better had!

EVA. Promise not stop me.

LIL. No promises. Truth.

EVA. Please . . .

LIL. Now!

EVA. Out walking.

LIL. Where?

EVA. Streets. Knocking on doors.

LIL. What doors?

EVA. Big houses. Rich people.

LIL. Eva!

EVA. I say about (*Pronouncing very carefully*) Butler and
    Housekeeper and Chauffeur and Gardener.

LIL. And what do they say?

EVA. 'We have already got.' Or some want to give tea and be
    sorry. Gentleman gave money at me.

LIL. The shame of it. What on earth d'you think we put an ad
    in for! To pass the time and have a laugh?

EVA. Sorry.

LIL. Don't you trust me! What good is it if you don't bloody trust me.

EVA. Sorry.

LIL. I took you in didn't I! Said I'd look after you! Why'd you throw it back in my face! Walking the streets like some begging little orphan!

EVA. Do not throw me out. Please.

LIL. Of course, I'm not going to throw you out!

EVA. Please. Nowhere else to go.

LIL (*gentler*). Of course, I'm not going to throw you out.

EVA. Even if I'm naughty.

LIL. Not even if you're naughty.

   LIL *hugs* EVA.

EVA. Want to be with them.

LIL. You can't be. Not now.

EVA. When?

LIL. Sooner or later.

EVA. I have to get permits.

LIL. Just be glad you're safe.

EVA. What good me to be safe?

LIL. Better than no one being safe, isn't it?

EVA. I must to help . . .

LIL. You are doing.

EVA. But jobs . . .

LIL. . . . are being found for them.

   EVA *drops her head.*

   Be a bit patient won't you?

   EVA *shrugs.*

   Cheer up and give them out there good reason to be happy. Else what've they got to smile for?

EVA *shrugs.*

LIL. Well. What've they got?

EVA (*quietly. German*). Nichts.

LIL. What's that?

EVA (*louder. German*). Nichts. Nothing.

LIL. That's right, little getaway. Nothing.

EVA *exits.*

FAITH. Did Dad know about this?

LIL. Don't go telling him.

FAITH. He must have had some idea.

LIL. He had no reason to know any more than you did.

The door opens. EVELYN *enters.*

EVELYN. There's a beautifully laid table with a cold pot of tea on it in the kitchen.

LIL. We got waylaid.

EVELYN. Why are you both still in here? Come on out and I'll lock the door.

FAITH *does not move.*

LIL (*to* EVELYN). You go down. I'm just getting something sorted.

EVELYN. Can't you do that elsewhere? Come downstairs.

EVELYN *sees the toys.*

Oh Faith, what on earth have you been doing?

EVELYN *starts to tidy up the dolls.*

LIL. I told her to put them away.

EVELYN. It's probably far better if I deal with it.

FAITH. Why did you keep them?

EVELYN. I'm sorry?

FAITH. You used to throw them away as if they were rubbish.

EVELYN. I hardly think so, darling.

FAITH. It happened a few times.

EVELYN. Maybe once when you'd made a mess.

FAITH. I had to rescue them before the bin men came.

EVELYN. Did you?

FAITH. I was surprised to find them here.

EVELYN. You're still very good at making a mess aren't you Faith?

FAITH. I thought you'd thrown them away for good.

EVELYN. I wouldn't do that.

FAITH. I found a box of letters and photographs.

LIL. Let's boil up a fresh kettle.

FAITH. I don't want any tea.

LIL. Faith.

FAITH. I'm not going to lie or pretend that nothing has happened.

EVELYN. Darling, you really do not need to get so distressed about the smallest thing.

FAITH. I'm not as good at putting on an act as you are.

LIL (*tidying up the letters etc*). I'll put these away . . .

EVELYN. No, Mum, please. I'd much rather do it myself.

FAITH. I found this book too.

LIL. Watch yourself.

EVELYN *tidies up.*

FAITH. Don't you want to see the book?

EVELYN. We'd better have tea soon or it'll be time for dinner.

FAITH. You remember the story of the Ratcatcher, don't you? This must be your book. It's not at all like I imagined. It's in German.

LIL. No more, Faith.

FAITH. Mum, tell me about Eva Schlesinger.

EVELYN (*to* LIL). What have people been saying?

LIL (*to* EVELYN). Don't look at me.

EVELYN. Will you please put that book back where you found it.

FAITH. You don't have to keep anything hidden.

EVELYN. I'm not hiding.

FAITH. Talk to me.

EVELYN. There is nothing to talk about.

FAITH. Please tell me the truth about yourself.

EVELYN (*turning to* LIL). Mum?

LIL (*to* FAITH). You shouldn't have brought it up.

FAITH. I can't un-know it.

EVELYN. Whatever it is you think you've discovered. You must forget it.

FAITH. Of course I can't forget it.

EVELYN. I certainly have.

FAITH. You do admit that you were Eva Schlesinger then?

EVELYN. What do you mean?

FAITH. You said you'd forgotten what I've discovered.

EVELYN. No I didn't . . . Did I? . . . No . . .

EVELYN *goes blank.*

FAITH. Mum?

EVELYN (*to* LIL). Why can't she respect my privacy?

LIL. I told her that she shouldn't have looked. (*To* FAITH.) Why can't you give over sometimes . . .

EVELYN. It's perfectly alright.

FAITH. Are you OK Mum?

EVELYN. We'll all agree to let it be . . .

FAITH. Are you saying that I should pretend along with you?

EVELYN (*looking at the papers and photos*). Mum, would you mind putting them all away?

LIL (*clearing up*). I don't know why you had to hold onto it all anyway.

EVELYN. They need sifting. I never could . . . There's some documents in there . . . I have to keep those . . . the rest needed throwing away years ago.

FAITH. You mustn't throw them away. Let me have them.

EVELYN (*to* FAITH). I don't want you getting involved with all that. No. (*To* LIL.) She mustn't. It's got nothing to do with her.

FAITH. It has got something to do with me.

EVELYN. It has got nothing to do with you at all.

FAITH. I just want to know about you.

EVELYN. You do know about me.

FAITH. And my grandparents.

LIL (*to* EVELYN). You'll have to talk to her.

EVELYN. I think, Faith, that this conversation must come to a close.

FAITH. Don't do this, Mother. You always do this. It only makes things worse.

EVELYN. We cannot continue to discuss the subject profitably.

EVELYN *makes to exit.*

LIL. You can't leave it like this, Evelyn.

FAITH *leaps in front of her and bars the door.*

FAITH. I'm not letting it go.

EVELYN. What is wrong with you?

FAITH. Do you have any idea what it's like having a mother who walks out on you the moment you begin to disagree with her? Who polishes and cleans like a maniac?

EVELYN. Pull yourself together.

FAITH. Pull myself together? You're so paranoid you go stiff and sharp at every speck of dust or object out of place in your precious home . . .

EVELYN. I care about where I live. I know what it's worth.

FAITH. You can't go on a train without hyper-ventilating. You cross the road if you see a policeman or traffic warden.

EVELYN. How ridiculous.

FAITH. I've watched your panic attacks. All that shaking and gulping like you're going to die. But always it's me who's getting things out of proportion because I get scared by them. 'So silly and neurotic, Faith.'

EVELYN. Look at you now.

FAITH. I have never been a good enough daughter.

EVELYN. What are you going on about?

FAITH. I've always thought it was my fault that you were so unhappy.

EVELYN. I am not unhappy. Heavens knows why you are.

FAITH. Nothing I do or say ever gets through to you . . .

EVELYN. Don't talk such nonsense.

FAITH. Listen to me.

EVELYN. I am listening.

FAITH. All you've given me is a pack of lies.

LIL. Watch what you say, Faith.

EVELYN. I have never lied to you.

FAITH. Don't try making out I'm making this up. I've got proof. Look. Evidence. That's the truth. And you didn't ever tell it to me. Not any of it.

EVELYN. You're hysterical.

EVELYN *tries to leave again.*

FAITH *continues to block her way.*

FAITH. Jesus. How could I possibly not be a bad child with such a terrible mother!

LIL. That's enough.

FAITH. A fucking, awful, lying cow of a mother.

EVELYN. How dare you!

LIL. You don't know the half of it, madam. Give your mother some consideration.

FAITH. If someone would let me in on the whole of it, I might bloody well be able to!

EVELYN. Have you finished?

FAITH. Why did you never explain about yourself?

EVELYN. Have you quite finished?

FAITH. I could kill you.

LIL (*going for* FAITH). I'll bloody kill you first!

   FAITH *runs away.* LIL *follows her.*

   Pipe music. The shadow of the Ratcatcher looms.

EVA. He's coming.

EVELYN. Stop.

EVA. His eyes are sharp as knives.

EVELYN. Be quiet.

EVA. He'll cut off my nose.

EVELYN. He's not coming.

EVA. He'll burn my fingers till they melt.

EVELYN. You've not done anything wrong.

EVA. He'll pull out my hair one piece at a time.

EVELYN. You're a good girl.

EVA. Don't let him come. Please!

EVELYN. He won't come.

EVA. He will.

EVELYN. I promise. I won't let him. I'll do everything I can to stop him. You'll see. You're with me now. He can't touch me. Do you understand? I'm here. You're being looked after. I won't go away. I'll make it all disappear. I'll get rid of him. He won't take you anywhere ever again.

End of Act One.

ACT TWO

Scene One

The room is dim. The air is stale and smoke-filled.

EVELYN's clothes and hair are unkempt. Beside her is an ashtray containing a large number of cigarette stubs.

She lights her cigarette lighter and holds it in front of her like a candle. It illuminates two figures beside her.

HELGA *is sitting with 'The Rattenfanger' book. EVA curls into her.*

EVELYN *stares at the flame.*

HELGA (*to* EVA). Do you understand what I mean about your being my jewels?

EVA. That's not in the story.

HELGA. Do you understand?

EVA. Sort of.

HELGA. We all die one day, but jewels never fade or perish. Through our children we live. That's how we cheat death. Otherwise we're really finished.

EVA. You're not going to die are you?

HELGA. Not yet.

EVA. Not for a long time.

HELGA. I hope not.

EVA. Promise me.

HELGA. Promise me you'll be a good girl in England.

EVA. I promise.

EVELYN. Promise me.

A tap on the door. Pause. Another tap, louder. Pause.

FAITH (*off*). Mum.

   Pause.

FAITH (*off. Louder*). Mum! The door's still locked.

   Pause.

FAITH (*off*). Please let me in.

   Pause.

FAITH (*off*). Please, Mum.

EVELYN. I am not coming out.

FAITH (*off*). You can't just stay in there.

EVELYN. Can I not?

FAITH (*off*). What about dinner?

EVELYN. Eat without me.

FAITH (*off*). What about tonight?

EVELYN. Leave me alone.

FAITH (*off*). This is crazy.

   Pause.

FAITH (*off*). I'm sorry about what I said.

   Pause.

FAITH (*off*). Mum? Can you still hear me?

EVELYN. Go away.

FAITH (*off*). I'm worried about you.

EVELYN. It's too late.

   Pause.

FAITH (*off*). Mum.

EVELYN. I'm going to stop talking to you now.

FAITH (*off*). Shit!

   Silence.

EVELYN. I didn't bring you up to speak as if your mouth were filled with sewage.

EVELYN *looks anxiously at all the boxes in the room.*

EVELYN. What else? What else?

She starts opening boxes, looking inside them and pulling out the contents transforming the room into a mess.

She approaches the box of letters and photos and lights her lighter to it momentarily, then lights another cigarette instead. She surveys the room intensely, searching with her gaze.

A man's voice repeating 'Sieg Heil' is heard.

The postman enters. He is frog marching, making a Hitler moustache on his upper lip with the index finger of one hand and doing the Nazi salute with the other.

POSTMAN. Sieg Heil! Sieg Heil! Sieg Heil! Sieg Heil!

POSTMAN *takes out a parcel.* EVELYN's *gaze immediately fixes upon it.*

POSTMAN. German parcel delivered in ze German style.

POSTMAN *clicks his heels together, stands to attention and holds out the parcel.*

Pretty convincing, eh?

EVA. German peoples not do like the . . . (*Mimes the moustache.*)

POSTMAN. But the moustache is the most important thing about him.

EVA. You do fun. German people not do fun.

POSTMAN. No. They wouldn't.

POSTMAN *marches without the moustache.*

POSTMAN. What about the marching?

EVA. I not know how do marching.

POSTMAN. I thought everyone in Boche Land learnt to march. Children 'n' all.

EVA. Only some. Hitler Jugend.

POSTMAN. What's that?

EVA. Children army. I not in it.

POSTMAN. They must've taught you to 'Sieg Heil'?

EVA. In school. Do this.

She stands to attention and salutes.

'Heil Hitler!'

POSTMAN. Have to do that a lot, did you?

EVA. Too much.

POSTMAN. Not very fond of Hitler are you?

EVA. He not a good man.

POSTMAN. Thought he'd done wonderful things for your country.

EVA. Not for my family.

POSTMAN. Did you ever see him though?

EVA. See Hitler?

POSTMAN. Did you?

EVA. One time.

POSTMAN. Went to one of them rallies was it?

EVA. Not rally. In Hamburg city. He in car. Me on street. Lots people. They shout very loud.

POSTMAN. Did he smell?

EVA. Smell?

POSTMAN. Everyone knows he smells. All Germans smell. Well-known fact.

EVA. Not me.

POSTMAN. That's coz you've been here a bit. It's started to fade.

EVA (*smelling herself*). Girls in school in Hamburg say I smell.

POSTMAN. That's not very nice of them.

EVA. Which smells more, German or Jew?

POSTMAN. Same difference, love.

EVA. Thank you for the parcel.

POSTMAN. Thank you for the marching lesson. (*He salutes.*) Heil Hitler!

EVA *watches.*

POSTMAN. Do it back. Heil Hitler!

EVA. Heil Hitler!

POSTMAN *exits.* EVA *carefully unwraps the parcel.*

EVELYN. Of course.

EVELYN *lunges at a case and empties it of all the children's clothes carefully packed inside it. She checks each item.*

HELGA. To the very best daughter any parents could wish for. The jobs. The permits. Thank you.

EVA. It wasn't all me.

HELGA. You have opened the door to a new and hopeful life.

EVA. Mrs Miller did as much as I did.

HELGA. Not long now. And then all of us together again. As I promised.

EVA *takes out of the parcel Der Rattenfänger book, a letter and a Haggadah for Passover.*

EVELYN *unpacks and checks the clothes.*

HELGA. Your storybook. I know how much you like it.

EVA *opens the letter.*

HELGA. I also enclose your Haggadah for Passover.

EVA. When is Passover?

HELGA. I hear that there are lots of Jews in Manchester.

EVA. Is it before or after Easter?

HELGA. It will be easy to celebrate seder night with some of them.

EVA. Maybe it's happened already.

HELGA. We will be having a small seder. Not like the big ones we used to have.

EVA. I can't ask Mrs Miller to do a seder.

HELGA. 'Why is this night different from all other nights?' What will we do without you to sing the questions for us? What is a seder without the presence of the youngest child?

EVA. She'd think it was silly.

HELGA. We have never been a very religious family, Eva. But this has to do with more than religion.

EVA. Next year when they're here. I'll do it then.

HELGA. The Passover story has special meaning for us.

EVA. Maybe I could just read the Haggadah to myself. Would that count?

HELGA. Remember how the Israelites had to endure hard labour.

EVA. Some of it's quite boring though.

HELGA. How every son was thrown into the Nile.

EVA. The ten plagues upon the Egyptians is good.

HELGA. And Moses led the Israelites out of slavery and the waves of the Red Sea parted to let them through.

EVA. And when all the Egyptians follow into the path between the waves and get drowned. They deserved it.

HELGA. We must tell the story not as if it was experienced only by our ancestors but as if it happened to us. Not legend but truth. 'This is what happened to ME when I came out of Egypt.' This is how we survived and this is how we survive.

EVA. When did there stop being miracles?

HELGA. And remember the four sons: the wise son, the bad son, the stupid son and the son who doesn't even know what to ask.

EVELYN *pulls out the coat worn by* EVA *for her journey out of Germany.*

HELGA. Try to be like the wise son, Eva.

EVA. What if I can't be wise?

HELGA. The weather here is lovely at the moment. The garden is looking beautiful. I wish I could bring it all with me over to England.

EVA. Will I get led like the Egyptians into the sea and drown forever?

HELGA. I am so looking forward to seeing you again and meeting your lovely English family. All my love. Mutti.

Banging on the door.

LIL (*off*). Let me in, Evelyn. I won't go away until you do.

EVELYN. Let me be.

LIL (*off*). You've had far too much time to be. That's enough.

EVELYN. Please go away, Mum.

LIL (*off*). I'll call the fire brigade if I have to. I'll say that the door's jammed . . .

EVELYN. No!

LIL (*off*). I will!

EVELYN. Go away.

LIL (*off*). I'll go and phone them now if you like.

EVELYN *puts down the coat and goes to the door. She unlocks it.* LIL *enters.*

LIL. I gave her hell.

EVELYN *is silent.*

LIL. The state of this place.

EVELYN. It wasn't all in the box.

LIL. What else have you got hidden away?

EVELYN. I've found it now.

EVELYN *closes the door and locks it behind* LIL.

LIL. What are you doing?

EVELYN. I don't want anyone coming in.

LIL. There's no point locking the safe after the robber's been and gone.

EVELYN. I have to work out what to do.

LIL. How about airing this room for starters.

EVELYN *lights up a cigarette. She offers one to* LIL.

LIL. I'm not meant to.

EVELYN. Just one. Keep me company.

LIL. I thought you'd given up.

EVELYN. I have.

LIL. You're as bad as a walking ashtray, you . . .

EVELYN. Like mother like daughter.

LIL. You're a bad influence on me.

LIL *takes one and* EVELYN *lights it up.*

LIL. She didn't mean what she said. It's probably left overs from her dad going. You're here to blame.

EVELYN. She meant it.

Pause.

LIL. She's always been hyper-sensitive.

Pause. EVELYN *inhales deeply.*

LIL. I don't understand you.

EVELYN. Thought you knew me better than I know myself.

LIL. Not when you behave like this, I don't.

EVELYN. You think I'm paranoid too, do you?

LIL. I do at the moment.

EVELYN. Do you think I'm 'stiff and sharp' as well?

LIL. You can be.

EVELYN. A terrible mother?

LIL. Not usually.

EVELYN. In what way am I being a terrible mother?

LIL. Locking her out when you should look her in the eye.

EVELYN. Maybe I don't like what I see reflected.

LIL. Now you're being hyper-sensitive.

EVELYN. She hates me.

LIL. Why should she hate you? She's your daughter.

EVELYN. That's why she hates me.

LIL. Stuff and nonsense.

EVELYN. You heard the abuse she threw at me.

LIL. She was upset.

EVELYN. She'll never understand.

LIL. Let her get used to the idea.

EVELYN. She'll always blame me.

LIL. You've not done anything wrong.

EVELYN. We've all done something wrong.

LIL. Speak for yourself.

EVELYN. You told her.

LIL. She found those letters and photos and god knows what else. It didn't take a genius to put two and two together.

EVELYN. Who confirmed it?

LIL. What was I meant to do? Lie?

EVELYN. It's not necessary to lie.

LIL. You shouldn't have kept them.

EVELYN. That's not the point.

LIL. To be honest, Evelyn, I don't think it's such a big deal.

EVELYN. My daughter hates me and it's not a big deal?

LIL. You're the one who's making her hate you.

EVELYN. The whitewash has been stripped away and underneath is pure filth.

LIL. Now, you're making no sense at all.

EVELYN. The more she knows, the worse it gets.

LIL. It was a long time ago. It doesn't matter any more.

EVELYN. Oh. It matters.

LIL. You'll put yourself over the edge if you're not careful.

EVELYN. Where else is there to go?

Sounds of children's chatter and train noises.

EVA *very reluctantly puts a gas mask box on a string round her neck and picks up her small suitcase.*

EVA. Will you visit me?

LIL. I said, didn't I.

EVA. And you tell Mutti and Vati how to find me when they come?

LIL. What did I say, Eva. Don't you trust me?

EVA. I have to be sure.

LIL. Have you got everything?

EVA. Teacher's already checked me.

LIL. Let me check you again.

EVA. Why?

LIL. Why'd you think? To be sure. What you got?

EVA. Bag.

LIL. Just one?

EVA. Yes.

LIL. Gas mask?

EVA. Yes.

LIL. Sandwiches?

EVA. Yes.

LIL. You're not wearing that jewellery are you?

EVA. I have to.

LIL. Anything could happen to it.

EVA. I'm not taking it off.

LIL. Give it me. I'll take it home . . .

EVA. I'm not taking it off.

LIL. Keep it on then. I haven't got the energy for a fight.

Train whistle blows.

LIL. Better get a move on.

LIL *takes out a label.*

EVA. Why do I have to go now? There's no war.

LIL. It could start any time. All the children's going. We can tie it to your button hole.

EVA. Mummy Miller . . .

LIL. Where shall we put it then?

EVA. I saw someone on the platform.

LIL. Who?

EVA. He's coming to get me.

LIL. Who is?

EVA. He's waiting in the shadows.

LIL. There's no one there.

EVA. Don't make me go.

LIL. Nora and Margaret's going with their classes aren't they? It's not just you being evacuated. All the children have got to go. You'll be a heck of a lot safer out of the city. Keep still now. I can't get a grip.

EVA (*looking around*). Let me go tomorrow.

LIL. I said. There could be war any day. D'you want to be bombed to bits, gassed till you choke?

EVA. I might never come back.

LIL. It's my job to care about what happens to you, even if you don't.

EVA. But . . .

LIL. I want you safe and out of it.

EVA. But what about you and Uncle Jack?

LIL. Don't you worry about us.

EVA. But I do.

LIL. You'll thank me one day. (*Finishing the label.*) It's on! Right . . . Bye bye, lovie . . .

They hug. EVA *clings on.*

LIL. Let go now.

EVA. Don't want to.

LIL *pulls herself away from* EVA *and puts her on the train.*

LIL. It's for your own good.

EVA. I'd rather get bombed.

LIL. I'll visit you at the weekend.

EVA looks very miserable and starts to wave.

Whistle blows again.

Sounds of train about to start to move.

EVA. We've got to stop! He'll take us over the edge. Got to get away from him. (*She starts to choke and cough.*)

EVELYN starts coughing.

Sounds of train moving.

EVA. This can't happen! It mustn't happen! Help! Leave me alone! Leave me alone! Help!

EVA leaps and lands with a roll, then lies still.

LIL (*off*). Eva! Eva Schlesinger!

EVA raises her head. She is dazed.

EVA. Am I in the abyss?

LIL. You're with me.

EVA. Did I get away?

LIL. And how.

EVA. Has the Ratcatcher gone?

LIL. There's no Ratcatcher here.

EVA. Are you sure?

LIL. He's a long way away.

EVA. He didn't get me.

LIL. Have you broken anything?

EVA (*sitting up slowly*). Don't think so.

LIL. You didn't hit your head.

EVA. Are you cross?

LIL. Cross! (*Realising she isn't.*) No. (*She pauses.*) I'm sorry.

EVA. You're sorry?

LIL. Should've realised. Shouldn't have made you go.

EVA. The ground was moving.

LIL. It isn't what you need most.

EVA. Couldn't keep my balance.

LIL (*helping EVA take off her gas mask*). I didn't want you to go. More than Margaret and Nora. Don't know why.

EVA. You didn't say.

LIL. Didn't want to upset you. If I'd clung, you would've done. Can you get up?

EVA. Have I been very bad?

LIL. No. Eva. I'm the one who got it wrong.

LIL *helps* EVA *up.*

EVELYN. What shall I do with the papers?

LIL. You should've known she'd find them one day.

EVELYN. She's never searched in here in her life.

LIL. Burying's not enough, love. You have to destroy.

EVELYN. How could I destroy them? There are documents in there that prove I have a right to be here. Papers that will stop them from sending me away.

LIL. Who'd want to send you away?

EVELYN. Someone. Anyone. You can never tell. Who knows what they may be thinking.

LIL. Who for god's sake!

EVELYN. The authorities.

LIL. Your passport's not in there is it?

EVELYN. Not my current one.

LIL. And your naturalisation papers?

EVELYN. The first entry permit is. There might be other documents.

LIL. Dig them out then.

EVELYN. I don't want to touch those letters and pictures.

LIL. I'll help.

EVELYN *pulls back.*

LIL. Don't you trust me?

EVELYN. Yes.

LIL. I'll sort them out with you.

LIL brings the box of papers over and takes out a letter. She holds it out to EVELYN.

LIL. Do you want to keep this?

EVELYN *looks at the letter.*

LIL. It's personal not official.

EVELYN. No.

LIL. What shall I do with it?

EVELYN (*taking it*). I'll rip it up.

EVELYN *holds it.*

LIL. If you're going to do it, do it.

EVELYN *is still.*

What're you waiting for? Get tearing.

EVELYN *looks at the paper.*

LIL. Go on.

EVELYN. Why are you so keen for me decimate everything?

LIL. I thought you wanted shot of it.

EVELYN. I do . . . I just . . .

LIL. Here love, let me.

EVELYN. No.

LIL. If you can't, I will.

EVELYN. It's mine not yours.

LIL. Don't be so daft.

EVELYN. You've always done too much.

LIL. How could I ever do enough?

EVELYN. You took too much.

LIL. How did I take?

EVELYN. Too much of me. You took me away.

LIL. What d'you mean by that?

EVELYN. I wasn't your child.

LIL. As good as . . .

EVELYN. You made me betray her.

LIL. I got you through it. Never forget that, Evelyn.

EVELYN. You made me betray them all.

LIL. I was with you and I put up with you and I stuck by you.
    That's what mothering's all about. Being there when it
    counts. No one else was there, were they? And good or bad,
    I'm still here. Who else have you got?

EVELYN. No one.

LIL. That's right, Evelyn, no one.

EVELYN. And isn't that what you always wanted?

LIL. Did I start the war? Am I Hitler?

EVELYN. You might as well have been.

LIL. What have I done to you that wasn't done in love?

EVELYN. What are you? Some saint? . . .

LIL. I didn't have to take you in . . .

EVELYN. Some saviour to all the world's poor little orphans?

LIL. I could've starved you or worked you . . .

EVELYN. And what do I have to pay?

LIL. I could've hit you . . .

EVELYN. What's your price?

LIL. I saved you.

EVELYN. Part of me is dead because of you.

LIL. Nothing you say will make me walk out that door.

EVELYN. Murderer.

LIL. I kept you alive. More than alive.

EVELYN. Child-stealer.

LIL. Go on then. Bare your grudges at me. What else do you
    want to blame me for? What other ills in your life are all
    down to me?

EVELYN. Shut up.

LIL. I'm waiting.

EVELYN. I don't want to blame you.

LIL. What do you want?

EVELYN. I want it never to have happened.

LIL. Well it did.

   Pause.

LIL. Now what?

EVELYN. Enough.

   EVELYN *tears up the letter into small pieces. She and* LIL
   proceed to destroy each item in the box.

STATION GUARD *enters.*

GUARD (*to* EVA). Can I help you, love?

EVA. What?

GUARD. You waiting for someone?

EVA. Two people.

GUARD. What do they look like, love?

EVA *takes out a photo and shows it.*

GUARD. Well-heeled.

EVA. Mother knows a good cobbler.

GUARD. Right. Is that them?

EVA. No.

GUARD. They your parents are they?

EVA. Yes.

They look.

GUARD (*pointing*). What about those two?

EVA. No.

GUARD. You're not here on your own to meet them are you?

EVA. Mrs Miller has just gone to cloakroom.

GUARD. Who's that then?

EVA. She looks after me.

GUARD. She knows where to find you?

EVA. Oh yes.

GUARD. What about that woman there?

EVA. No.

GUARD. Live in Manchester do you?

EVA. Yes.

GUARD. Not been evacuated then?

EVA. No.

They look.

GUARD. Well, I'm afraid they don't seem to be here, your Mam and Dad.

EVA. They will come.

GUARD. You sure they were on this train?

EVA. They write that they come to me on September 9th.

GUARD. But, it's September 11th today.

EVA. They must to come soon.

GUARD. Look. Are you certain they were travelling from London?

EVA. Yes . . . it must be . . . I got here from there.

GUARD. You see there's no more trains today from London.

EVA. Are you sure?

GUARD. Course I am.

EVA. It can't be.

GUARD (*suspicious*). Where are you from?

EVA. 72 Mulberry Road . . .

GUARD. No. I mean, what's your nationality?

EVA. My?

GUARD. What country you from?

EVA (*worried*). I don't live there any more.

GUARD. Where don't you live any more?

EVA. It does not matter so much.

GUARD. And where's this lady who's looking after you? She's left you a long time on your own hasn't she?

EVA. I don't know.

GUARD. (*taking her by the arm*). I think that you'd better come with me young lady.

    LIL *runs up to* EVA.

LIL. Eva! Eva! Where the hell did you go!

GUARD. Are you supposed to be looking after her?

LIL. I just went to the cloakroom.

GUARD. You should take better care of her. Can't leave a girl of her age on her own. Specially nowadays. Could be an air raid warning any minute.

LIL. She ran off. (*To* EVA.) What d'you do that for? You had me frantic. D'you think I like pacing platforms looking for you!

GUARD. And what's this about her being a foreigner?

LIL (*to* EVA). The last train's been and gone, love.

EVA. We cannot to give up yet.

LIL. We've been here three days on the trot.

EVA. Please can we come back tomorrow.

LIL. I don't think they're coming. (*To* GUARD.) I'll take her now.

GUARD. I asked you about her being a foreigner?

LIL (*to* GUARD). Don't worry yourself about it.

GUARD. Got to look out for spies we have.

LIL. She's not a spy. She's ten years old.

GUARD. What about them parents she's waiting for?

LIL. Her parents are still in Germany.

EVA. No, they're not!

GUARD. Are they indeed?

LIL. Just leave it to me, will you. (*To* EVA.) I did warn you that this would happen.

GUARD. What's she doing here then? She should be in Germany with them.

EVA. Maybe they're in London.

LIL. Eva. They're not coming.

EVA. They keep their promises. Always.

LIL. Wars break promises.

EVA. They must be coming some different way. They have their visas got by now . . . they have written to us that they come this week . . .

LIL. They wrote that before the war started. If it'd broke out a fortnight later . . .

EVA. I want them to come. I got permits!

LIL. Believe me, Eva love, I want them to come too.

GUARD. Well, I don't.

EVA. You are wrong! You are wrong! They will come!

LIL. There's no way through.

EVA. There is!

LIL. There isn't.

GUARD. If they put one foot into this country, they'll be interned straight off. Got to protect ourselves.

EVA. No!

LIL. Oh Eva.

EVA. No! No! No! No! No!

LIL. I know. I know.

EVA. No!

   EVA *shakes with distress.*

GUARD (*exiting*). Should've stayed where she belongs.

LIL. We can go to Church and pray for them.

EVA. I don't know how to pray in a church.

LIL. It's a lot easier to learn than English.

EVA. I'll never see them again, will I?

LIL. They've got as much chance of surviving as we have. And I'm not dying and neither are you.

   EVA *takes off two rings, a charm bracelet, a watch and a chain with a Star of David on it.*

EVELYN *takes off her watch.*

LIL. What're you doing?

EVA. I don't want to wear these any more.

LIL (*to* EVA). Why on earth not?

EVA. I don't like them.

LIL. We'll put them away safe at home.

EVA. How much longer can I stay with you?

LIL. Don't ask stupid questions.

LIL *takes* EVA's *arm and leads her away.*

EVELYN. Are we still tearing?

EVELYN *rips.* LIL *picks up 'Der Rattenfänger' book and starts to tear out the first page.*

EVELYN. No. Not that.

LIL. It's in German. Horrible pictures.

EVELYN. You can't damage a book. I'll give it to a second hand shop.

LIL (*picking up the Haggadah*). What about this?

EVELYN. That too.

EVELYN *puts the books to the side.* LIL *opens a letter.*

EVELYN *picks up the mouth organ. She doesn't recognise it. She puts it with the books.*

LIL *reads the letter in her hand intently.*

EVELYN. Is it important?

LIL. It's them changing their mind about letting you stay on at school after we fought them . . .

EVELYN. Rip it up.

LIL. 'We accept Eva's proven brilliancy . . .'

EVELYN. Mum.

LIL. Can't we save it?

EVELYN. What did you say about destroying?

LIL. It's so complimentary about you . . .

EVELYN. Give it to me.

EVELYN *takes it and tears it.*

You were absolutely right. All this unpleasantness could have been avoided. I should have sifted through all these years ago. It's only paper. It tears so easily.

LIL. Too easily.

EVELYN. Are you backing off?

LIL. Not at all.

EVELYN. What's done is done, Mum.

LIL. But not everything . . .

EVELYN. There must be nothing left to drag me down.

LIL. I'd only like something . . .

EVELYN. Nothing.

LIL. If you feel that strongly . . .

EVELYN. Let's let life go on shall we?

LIL. Better that than giving up, I suppose.

EVELYN. I absolutely refuse to give up.

LIL. I suppose you're a survivor.

EVELYN. Is that what I am? I must be. Yes. No matter what happens, no matter what anyone anywhere does. No matter how the skies may blaze and the earth tremble, it must continue. Mundane, ordinary life. Most people don't begin to know the value of it.

LIL. We'll both get over this.

EVELYN. Of course we will.

LIL. You've got over worse.

EVELYN. I've made a good life. All I can do is live it and count my blessings.

LIL. And make up with your daughter.

EVELYN. We'll see.

LIL. You always have to make an effort with your children. No matter what.

EVELYN. All our children leave us. And one day they never come back. I can't stop her.

LIL. You and I have been close.

EVELYN. You and I are different.

LIL. She's more like you than you think.

EVELYN. I don't want her to be like me.

LIL. She's herself too. Every child's their own person.

EVELYN. Was I?

LIL. And how.

EVELYN. Not any more. The older I get the less of myself I become.

LIL. The things you come out with.

EVELYN. I always knew she'd go. Didn't the German woman realise that too?

LIL. You mean your first mother?

EVELYN. She wanted me to be hers forever.

LIL. I thought you'd forgotten her.

EVELYN. It doesn't matter. I have.

EVELYN *continues to tear.*

Soundtrack of the newsreel about the liberation of Belsen.

LIL *and* EVA (*now fifteen*) *watch. Suddenly* LIL *throws a handkerchief over* EVA's *face and bundles her away.*

LIL. They should have a warning about what's in them newsreels. No children should see such pictures.

EVA (*taking the handkerchief off her face*). I'm not a child. I'm fifteen.

LIL. Especially not you. No matter how old you are.

EVA. It can't be kept from me forever.

LIL. D'you want to go back in then?

Pause.

EVA. No.

LIL. What you don't see can't come back to haunt you.

EVA. Everything went blank.

LIL. Thank God for handkerchieves.

EVA. The soldiers had them over their noses and mouths.

LIL. Don't think of it.

EVA. Can a handkerchief keep out the smell of all those bodies?

LIL. It couldn't hold all the tears that want crying.

Pause.

EVA. I don't want to cry.

LIL. Far too shocking.

EVA. Should I want to cry? Is it callous of me?

LIL. You react as you react.

EVA. We can still go in to see the main feature, can't we?

LIL. Do you want to?

EVA. Yes. Is that wrong?

LIL. It was our treat.

EVA. There's no reason why we should miss our treat is there? I mean, it wouldn't make any difference to anything else would it?

LIL. Sure you're in the mood?

EVA. I have been looking forward to it.

LIL. I don't know if I'm in the mood now.

EVA. You've already paid for the tickets and we won't have another chance before it finishes.

LIL. Alright.

Knocking on the door.

FAITH (off). Gran? Mum?

EVELYN *shakes her head.*

LIL. Go on down, Faith, love.

FAITH (*off*). What are you doing?

LIL. Let me sort it out.

FAITH (*off*). Let me in.

LIL. We'll be out soon. Promise.

FAITH (*off*). How soon?

LIL. Not long.

FAITH (*off*). I'll wait here.

EVA *stands on a box.* LIL *starts to fix her skirt hem.*

EVA. Thank you for helping.

LIL (*to* EVA). You can do your own hem next time.

EVA. You know I'm no good at sewing.

LIL. You'll have to learn sooner or later.

EVA (*taking the gold watch and jewellery out of her pocket*). How much d'you think they're worth?

LIL. What's worth?

EVA. Two rings. A charm bracelet. Gold. A chain with a Star of David. A watch. All gold.

LIL. Don't ask me. I'm not a jeweller.

EVA. It'd be quite a lot, wouldn't it?

LIL. Depends on the carat.

EVA. How d'you tell?

LIL. The hall mark.

EVA *peers at the jewellery.*

LIL. Why d'you want to know?

EVA. I was thinking of selling them.

LIL. What d'you want to sell them for?

EVA. I never wear them.

LIL. But they're beautiful, those. No one ever gave me jewellery like that.

EVA. I never will wear them either.

LIL. You should do.

EVA. I'm fed up of hiding the watch under my socks to stop hearing the ticking at night.

LIL. Those are priceless.

EVA. I'd rather have the money.

LIL. Money's nothing. You purse it, you spend it. Those are more. Family heirlooms. You want to be handing them down to your children.

EVA. I'd rather hand down things I feel happy about.

LIL. It's bad luck to sell a keepsake.

EVA. If they're mine, I can do what I want with them.

LIL. Are they yours?

EVA. My mother from Germany gave them to me.

LIL. To look after for her or have for yourself?

EVA. Same difference now.

LIL. We're still trying to track them down, aren't we? Still writing all those letters. Why are you so keen to give up?

EVA. It was all over a long time ago.

LIL. It isn't over till you know for sure.

EVA. I do know for sure.

LIL. Miracles can happen.

EVA. I don't believe in miracles.

LIL. It sounds to me like you don't want to.

EVA. I will sell them, Mum. There's better things the money could be spent on.

LIL. Like what?

EVA. To help me carry on at school . . .

LIL. Hey you, we sorted all that out . . .

EVA. I know, but we still have to pay for my school uniform and books and everything. I want to help out. Nora's earning now. I'm not.

LIL. Don't do it for me. I've never expected a penny off you. I had enough of that when I was a kid – Mam putting us out to work the minute she could, taking bed and board. I don't want your money.

EVA. I want to pay my way for myself as much as I can.

LIL. And I want to keep you. Like no one ever kept me. I don't care if it's hard. I'll do right by you. Somebody has to in this godforsaken world.

EVA. You've already done more than alright by me.

LIL. I've not finished yet.

EVA. D'you mind if I go now?

LIL. Just make sure no one diddles you.

Knocking on the door.

FAITH (*off*). Let me in. Please, let me in.

EVELYN *nods.* LIL *opens the door.* FAITH *enters.*

FAITH. My god.

EVELYN. We're going to clean this room up now.

FAITH. I didn't mean to shout at you like that.

EVELYN. It's over and done with.

FAITH. I'm sorry.

EVELYN. It's forgotten.

LIL *tidies around the box of torn papers.*

FAITH. What are those?

EVELYN. I've put an end to the trouble.

FAITH. You've torn up those letters and photos . . .

EVELYN. It's the only way forward.

FAITH (*to* LIL). How could you let her do this?

LIL. It's what we both think is best.

FAITH *kneels down and stares at the pieces. She tries to gather and fit them together.*

EVELYN. Don't get yourself all worked up now darling.

FAITH. Weren't these family documents . . . I mean . . . more than that . . . historical documents?

EVELYN. I know what they were.

LIL (*to* EVELYN). No one's accusing you, love.

FAITH. But . . . weren't these things . . . sort of . . . entrusted to you? Why didn't you look after them?

EVELYN *is silent.*

FAITH. Why didn't you pass them on to me?

EVELYN. I can do what I want with my own property.

FAITH. But how do I know what went before without them? How does anyone know? What proof is there? It could all be make-believe, couldn't it?

LIL (*to* FAITH). You're not doing a very good job of making up, Faith.

FAITH (*picking up scraps of paper from the floor*). Look at these remains. Where's the body for these feet? The hand for these fingers?

EVELYN. You know, Faith, there are hundreds of books on the subject. Read some of those if you must have a morbid interest in past events.

FAITH. Now they're just numbers lost in the millions. Who's going to be able to take care of their memory?

EVELYN. Are you going to go on at me about this for the rest of our lives?

FAITH. Did they die for you to forget?

EVELYN. Why are you being so cruel?

FAITH. Destroying these was crueller.

EVELYN. Do you think I don't know that.

FAITH. Why did you do it then?

EVELYN. Because – and I don't expect you to begin to understand this – it helps me. It gives me something I can do in
the face of it all.

FAITH. It can't change what happened though, can it?

EVELYN. Do you want to draw blood?

FAITH. Not blood.

EVELYN. Well, blood is all I have left. Gallons and gallons of
the freezing stuff stuck in my veins. One prick, Faith, and I
might bleed forever.

FAITH. Mother, don't . . .

EVELYN. Do you still want to know about my childhood,
about my origins, about my parents?

FAITH. Yes.

EVELYN. Well, let me tell you. Let me tell you what little
remains in my brain. And if I do, will you leave me alone
afterwards. Will you please leave me alone?

FAITH. If that's what you want . . .

EVELYN. My father was called Werner Schlesinger. My
mother was called Helga. They lived in Hamburg. They
were Jews. I was an only child. I think I must have loved
them a lot at one time. One forgets what these things feel
like. Other feelings displace the original ones. I remember a
huge cone of sweets that I had on my first day at school.
There were a lot of toffees.

She goes blank for a moment.

I remember lots of books. Rows and rows . . . a whole house
built of books and some of them were mine. A storybook
filled with terrifying pictures . . . children's fingers being cut
off, children whose teeth fall out and choke them while

they're asleep, children being burnt in attic rooms and no
one hearing them scream . . . Flames. Little flames flickering
in a holder with lots of arms. Silver arms and one twisted,
rocking leg holding them up. Old and faded. Rubbed away
in patches. Wobbly candles which wouldn't stand straight,
sticking out at strange angles. And one time . . . only once . . .
being allowed to light them. Even striking the match myself.
Just one, single time. And keeping watch while they melted
to nothing in case they burned the house down . . . which
would have been my fault because I lit them. The candles
were all different colours. The little lights were the most
beautiful . . . Silly lights . . . Silly, silly lights . . .

FAITH. Were they for something special?

EVELYN. The only other thing is a boy with a squint on the
train I came away on. I kept trying not to look at him. Please
believe me, Faith, there is nothing else in my memory from
that time. It honestly is blank.

FAITH. What happened to your parents?

EVELYN. They died.

FAITH. In a concentration camp?

EVELYN. Yes.

FAITH. Do you know which one?

EVELYN. Auschwitz.

LIL. When did you find that out?

FAITH. When did they die?

EVELYN. My father died in 1943. He was gassed soon after
arrival.

FAITH. What about your mother?

EVELYN. My mother . . . she was . . . she was not gassed.

FAITH. What happened to her?

HELGA *enters. She is utterly transformed – thin, wizened,
old-looking. Her hair is thin and short.*

HELGA. Ist das Eva? (Is it Eva?).

EVA *is speechless.*

HELGA. Eva, bist du's wirklich? (Is that you, Eva?)

EVA. Mother?

> HELGA *approaches* EVA *and hugs her.* EVA *tries to hug back but is clearly very uncomfortable.*

HELGA. Wie du dich verändert hast! (How much you have changed!)

EVA. I'm sorry. I don't quite understand.

HELGA. How much you have changed.

EVA. So have you.

HELGA. You are sixteen now.

EVA. Seventeen.

HELGA. Blue is suiting to you. A lovely dress.

EVA. Thank you.

HELGA. You are very pretty.

EVA. This is a nice hotel. I can't believe you're here.

HELGA. I promised I would come, Eva.

EVA. I'm called Evelyn now.

HELGA. What is Evelyn?

EVA. I changed my name.

HELGA. Why?

EVA. I wanted an English name.

HELGA. Eva was the name of your great grandmother.

EVA. I didn't mean any disrespect.

HELGA. No. Of course not.

EVA. I'm sorry.

HELGA. Nothing is the same any more.

EVA. It's just that I've settled down now.

HELGA. These are the pieces of my life.

EVA. There were no letters for all those years and then I saw the newsreels and newspapers . . .

HELGA. I am putting them all back together again.

EVA. I thought the worst.

HELGA. I always promised that I would come and get you.

EVA. I was a little girl then.

HELGA. I am sorry that there has been such a delay. It was not of my making.(*Pause.*) I am your mutti, Eva.

EVA. Evelyn.

HELGA. Eva. Now I am here, you have back your proper name.

EVA. Evelyn is on my naturalisation papers.

HELGA. Naturalised as English?

EVA. And adopted by Mr and Mrs Miller.

HELGA. How can you be adopted when your own mother is alive for you?

EVA. I thought that you were not alive.

HELGA. Never mind it. We have all done bad things in the last years that we regret. That is how we survive.

EVA. What did you do?

HELGA. I was right to send you here, yes? It is good to survive. Is it not, Eva?

EVA. Please call me Evelyn.

HELGA. Now we must put our lives right again. We will go to New York where your Onkel Klaus will help us to make a beginning.

EVA. All the way to New York?

HELGA. Who is here for us? No one. The remains of our family is in America.

EVA. I have a family here.

HELGA. These people were just a help to you in bad times.
    You can to leave them now behind. The bad times are
    finished. I know it.

EVA. I like it here.

HELGA. You will like it better in America.

EVA. Do I have to go away with you?

HELGA. That is what I came for.

Ratcatcher music.

Scene Two

*The torn papers and their box have been cleared away. The
rest of the room is still somewhat messed up.*

HELGA, *holding a suitcase, stands in a corner.*

EVELYN *has open the box of glasses. She rubs one with a tea
towel.*

FAITH *watches.*

EVELYN (*holding up a glass*). Will these be of any use?

FAITH. Aren't they a bit precious?

EVELYN. You can have them if you want them.

FAITH. If you're sure . . .

EVELYN. Yes or no?

FAITH. Yes.

EVELYN. Good. That's glasses done.

    FAITH *picks up the box and puts it by the door.*

    EVELYN *moves on to another box.*

    LIL *enters. She is wearing a coat.*

LIL. I'm off out now.

EVELYN. Will you be back for dinner?

LIL. Yes.

FAITH. Do you want me to give you a lift to the station tomorrow?

EVELYN. I said that I would.

FAITH. You hate driving into town.

LIL (*to* FAITH). I told her she didn't have to.

EVELYN (*to* LIL). I want to take you to the station.

LIL. You don't need to make anything up to me. I told you. It's alright.

EVELYN. Maybe I feel less alright about it than you do.

LIL. Don't be silly.

EVELYN. Just let me take you.

LIL. Alright, take me.

EVELYN. I'll find out about departure times.

LIL. I've already got a timetable.

EVELYN. Fine.

LIL. See you later then.

EVELYN. See you later.

FAITH. Bye.

　　LIL *exits.*

　　FAITH *starts to search through some boxes.*

EVELYN. Don't you do a thing. You'll only cause a muddle. (*Opening a box.*) Do you need cutlery?

FAITH. What sort?

EVELYN (*pushing the box to her*). Look at it and decide.

FAITH. This is silver.

EVELYN. I don't like it.

FAITH. Why not?

EVELYN. The design's far too fussy.

FAITH. I like it.

EVELYN. Take it.

FAITH. Thanks.

EVELYN. Not at all.

FAITH *puts the box by the door.*

EVELYN *continues to check boxes.*

FAITH. Gran didn't know that your mother survived did she?

EVELYN. If she had known, she would have made me go with her.

FAITH. To New York?

EVELYN. She would have handed me back like a borrowed package.

FAITH. She might not.

EVELYN. You know your gran as well as I do, Faith.

FAITH. Did you ever see her after she left?

EVELYN. No.

FAITH. Was she still alive when I was born?

EVELYN. Yes.

FAITH. When did she die?

EVELYN. In 1969.

FAITH. She lived a long time.

EVELYN. She was a very strong woman.

FAITH. Didn't you ever want to be with her?

EVELYN. We didn't get on.

FAITH. You stopped her from knowing me.

EVELYN. I have tried to do my best for you. Please believe that.

FAITH. You stopped me from knowing her.

EVELYN. I wish it could have been simpler. But it wasn't.

FAITH. I just feel that I've lost out on so much.

EVELYN. Don't hanker after the past. It's done.

FAITH. It's still a part of our lives.

EVELYN. It is an abyss.

FAITH. Before, all I knew was a blank space. Now, it's beginning to fill up. I have a background, a context.

EVELYN. All you have now is a pile of ashes.

FAITH. There's far more than ashes, Mum.

EVELYN (*opening out two boxes*). Crockery?

FAITH (*looking at it*). It's beautiful.

EVELYN. A collection.

FAITH. Why don't you use it.

EVELYN. I prefer the Royal Crescent set downstairs. That's an old fancy. I've outgrown it.

FAITH. I'll probably break it all.

EVELYN. I hope you won't.

FAITH. I was joking.

EVELYN. You will take care of this home of yours won't you?

FAITH. Of course, I will.

EVELYN. Do you have enough storage space?

FAITH. There's lots of empty cupboards.

Pause.

FAITH. Am I Jewish?

EVELYN. You've been baptized.

FAITH. Wouldn't the Nazis have said that I was Jewish?

EVELYN. You can't let people who hate you tell you what you are.

FAITH. I want to know what being Jewish means.

EVELYN. I'm afraid that I can't help.

FAITH. Don't you feel at all Jewish?

EVELYN. I was baptized when I was eighteen. I was cleansed that day. Purified.

FAITH. How can you say that?

EVELYN. I have truly been a great deal happier for it.

FAITH. What about being German?

EVELYN. Germany spat me out. England took me in. I love this place: the language, the countryside, the buildings, even the food. I danced and sang when I got my first British passport. I was so proud of it. My certificate of belonging. You can't imagine what it was like.

FAITH. It's hard starting from scratch.

EVELYN. You don't have to. You can carry on from where you are.

FAITH. Where I am has changed a lot in the last week.

Pause.

EVELYN. There's a portable television somewhere.

FAITH. This is what you're best at.

EVELYN. What is?

FAITH. Providing for me.

EVELYN. You're hardly able to do it all for yourself yet.

FAITH. I think I'll manage.

EVELYN. Not in the manner to which you have always been accustomed. (*Pulling out a desk lamp.*) What about a desk lamp?

FAITH. Does it work?

EVELYN. There's no bulb.

EVELYN. That's no problem.

FAITH *turns to pick up a box.*

EVELYN. I've got some spare ones in the kitchen cupboard . . .

FAITH. I'll start taking it all down.

EVELYN *pulls out the Haggadah and 'Der Rattenfänger' books.*

EVELYN *(holding them out to* FAITH*)*. There are these too.

FAITH *(putting down the box)*. You said everything had been destroyed.

EVELYN. They're just books. You might not want them . . .

FAITH *(taking the books)*. Of course I want them.

EVELYN. One is a storybook and the other is for some Jewish festival.

FAITH. Thank you.

EVELYN *picks up the mouth organ and coat.*

EVELYN. And these. They must have come with me.

FAITH *takes the mouth organ and coat. She holds up the coat and looks at it. She feels in the pockets.*

EVELYN. You'd better take that box down.

FAITH *pulls out a penny.*

FAITH. A penny.

EVELYN. Put it towards your own flat.

FAITH *puts the penny into her own pocket.*

FAITH *(holding out the coat to* EVELYN*)*. Why don't you keep the coat, Mum.

EVELYN *(identifying a box)*. Is this the one you want first?

FAITH *lays the coat away from her boxes and picks one up.*

EVELYN. Leave it to the left of the door in the hallway, not the right.

FAITH *picks up a box and exits.*

EVELYN *carefully sorts through boxes.*

Sounds of a quayside. A boat is about to leave.

EVA *enters.*

HELGA. Where have you been?

EVA. I said. In the lavatory.

HELGA. For half an hour in the lavatory?

EVA. I was being sick.

HELGA. Sick?

EVA. I'm alright now.

HELGA. Are you sure?

EVA. Yes.

HELGA. You should change your mind and come with me.

EVA. I haven't got a case.

HELGA. You could have your things sent on.

EVA. You said it was alright to come later.

HELGA. I said I would prefer you to come now. There is enough money from Onkel Klaus for a ticket.

EVA. I can't just leave.

HELGA. Why do you not want to be with your mother, Eva?

EVA. Evelyn. My name is Evelyn.

HELGA. Why are you so cold to me?

EVA. I don't mean to be cold.

HELGA. We have been together a week and you are still years away.

EVA. I can't help it.

Boat's hooter sounds.

HELGA. Boats do not wait for people.

EVA. I hope you have a safe trip.

HELGA. When is 'later' when you are coming?

EVA. In a month or two.

HELGA. Just get on the boat with me. Do it now.

EVA. I'm not ready yet. Not at all.

HELGA. You're making a mistake.

EVA. You're making me . . .

HELGA. What am I making you do! I am your mother. I love you. We must be together.

EVA. We've not been together for too long.

HELGA. That is why it is even more important now.

EVA. I can't leave home yet.

HELGA. Home is inside you. Inside me and you. It is not a place.

EVA. I don't understand what you mean.

HELGA. You are wasting a chance hardly anyone else has been given.

EVA. I will come.

HELGA. Will you?

EVA. If you want me to.

HELGA. If I want you to?

EVA. Just not yet.

HELGA. Do you want to come to make a new life with me?

EVA. You keep asking me that.

HELGA. Do you?

EVA. It's hard for me.

HELGA. I lost your father. He was sick and they put him in line for the showers. I saw it. You know what I say to you. I lost him. But I did not lose myself. Nearly, a million times over, right on the edge of life, but I held on with my bones rattling inside me. Why have you lost yourself, Eva?

Ship's horn sounds out.

HELGA. I am going to start again. I want my daughter Eva with me. If you find her, Evelyn, by any chance, send her over to find me.

HELGA *embraces* EVA *who stands stock still.*

HELGA *picks up her case and starts to walk away.*

EVELYN (*quietly*). There are four types of daughters: wise, bad, stupid and the ones who do not know what to ask.

HELGA (*turning round*). Which are you?

EVELYN. Don't look at the razor eyes. Whatever you do.

She looks at HELGA.

Why do you only ever stare at me like that? Are those the only eyes you have? Didn't you have others once? Eyes which didn't burn?

EVELYN. I wish you had died.

HELGA. I wish you had lived.

EVELYN. I did my best.

HELGA. Hitler started the job and you finished it.

EVELYN. Why does it have to be my fault?

HELGA. You cut off my fingers and pulled out my hair one strand at a time.

EVELYN. You were the Ratcatcher. Those were his eyes, his face . . .

HELGA. You hung me out of the window by my ears and broke my soul into shreds.

EVELYN. You threw me into the sea with all your baggage on my shoulders.

HELGA. You can never excuse yourself.

EVELYN. How could I swim ashore with so much heaviness on me? I was drowning in leagues and leagues of salty water.

HELGA. I have bled oceans out of my eyes.

EVELYN. I had to let go to float.

HELGA. Snake. Slithering out of yourself like it was an unwanted skin. Worm.

EVELYN. What right have you got to accuse me? You kept saying something. What was it? Over and over? Yes. 'No,' you said. That was all. 'No. I won't help you. You have to be able to manage on your own. Didn't you light the candles? Strike the match and it's time to go. You don't need me. See. It's good.' Was it really so very good, Mutti? Was it really what you wanted? It wasn't what I wanted. It was the last thing on this earth that I ever wanted . . .

HELGA. My suffering is monumental. Yours is personal.

EVELYN. Your suffering is a mountain. Mine is a tiny mound. How could I ever forget?

HELGA. How could you?

EVA *exits.*

EVELYN. What about what you did to me? (*She loses control.*) What right did you have to claim me back and hate me when I wouldn't come? You should have hung onto me and never let me go. Why did you send me away when you were in danger? No one made you. You chose to do it. Didn't it ever occur to you that I might have wanted to die with you. Because I did. I never wanted to live without you and you made me. What is more cruel than that? Except for coming back from the dead and punishing me for surviving on my own.

EVELYN *sobs.* FAITH *enters.*

FAITH (*to* EVELYN). Are you crying?

FAITH *tries to get close to* EVELYN. EVELYN *does not turn to face* FAITH.

FAITH. What can I do for you? Please tell me what I can do to help?

EVELYN. Stay my little girl forever.

FAITH. I can't.

EVELYN. Then there's nothing you can do.

FAITH. I'm going to find out what everything means. Get in touch with my relatives. I want to meet them.

EVELYN. You'll find them very different.

FAITH. I'm sure they'd love to see you too.

EVELYN. I have nothing in common with them and neither do you.

FAITH. I want to put that right.

EVELYN. I don't want you to bring trouble onto yourself.

FAITH. There won't be any trouble.

EVELYN. You don't know . . .

FAITH. We can do this together. It would make us closer to each other.

EVELYN. I'd rather die than go back.

FAITH. You might change your mind . . .

EVELYN. I can't.

HELGA *and* EVA *exit.*

FAITH (*going to another box*). Can I have my toys?

EVELYN. Surely you can leave those here.

FAITH. I want to take them with me.

EVELYN. I'd like to keep something from when you were little.

FAITH. They mean a lot to me.

EVELYN. Take them.

FAITH *picks up the box of toys.*

EVELYN. Have you got everything you need now?

FAITH. More or less.

EVELYN. All done in here then.

FAITH. Yes we are.

FAITH *exits.*

The coat lies in the attic.

The shadow of the Ratcatcher covers the stage.

The End.